OVERCOMING OBSESSIVE-COMPULSIVE DISORDER

■

A Behavioral and
Cognitive Protocol for
the Treatment of OCD

Gail Steketee, Ph.D.

BPT

Best Practices for Therapy

Empirically Based Treatment Protocols

Publisher's Note

This publication is designed to provide accurate and authoritative information in regard to the subject matter covered. It is sold with the understanding that the publisher is not engaged in rendering psychological, financial, legal, or other professional services. If expert assistance or counseling is needed, the services of a competent professional should be sought.

Distributed in the U.S.A. by Publishers Group West; in Canada by Raincoast Books; in Great Britain by Airlift Book Company, Ltd.; in South Africa by Real Books, Ltd.; in Australia by Boobook; and in New Zealand by Tandem Press.

Copyright © 1999 by Gail Steketee, Ph.D.
New Harbinger Publications, Inc.
5674 Shattuck Avenue
Oakland, CA 94609

Cover design by Poulson/Gluck Design.
Edited by Carole Honeychurch.
Text design by Michele Waters

Library of Congress Catalog Card Number: 98-67412
ISBN 1-57224-129-2 Paperback

Printed in the United States of America

New Harbinger Publications' Website address: www.newharbinger.com

02   01   00

10   9   8   7   6   5   4   3   2

Contents

Foreword

This client manual represents what I have learned from treating and supervising the treatment of hundreds of people with OCD, as well as information I have learned from many expert colleagues in this field. The behavioral treatment methods described here are based on many studies of behavioral methods; the cognitive therapy methods are based on only a few studies of cognitive therapy methods, and so these are considered more experimental. I thank my colleagues Sabine Wilhelm, Mark Freeston, Paul Salkovskis, and Patricia van Oppen for their insights into applying cognitive therapy to OCD problems and Lynn Bufka for helpful comments on an earlier draft.

I am grateful to OCD sufferers I have known for sharing their experience and struggling courageously during treatment to overcome their fears. I believe I have learned much from the opportunity to participate in their efforts to get better. Finally, I thank my husband, Brian, for his great patience in a time of overload to permit me to complete this manual.

Introduction

What Is Obsessive-Compulsive Disorder?

People who have obsessive-compulsive disorder (OCD) experience recurrent obsessions and/or compulsions that are severe enough to cause considerable distress and to interfere with the person's functioning at work, in social activities, in family and social relationships, or in everyday activities.

Obsessions are unwanted, intrusive thoughts, ideas, urges, impulses, or worries that run through a person's mind over and over again. Often the intrusive ideas are senseless, unpleasant, and quite distasteful; they produce fear, guilt, apprehension, sadness, or simply discomfort. Common obsessions include repeated impulses to kill a loved one; worries about dirt, germs, contamination, infection, and contagion; recurrent thoughts that something has not been done properly even when the individual knows it has; blasphemous thoughts or excessive concerns about following religious rules; sexual thoughts about doing something repugnant; fears of losing something important; ideas that certain things must always be in a certain place, position, or order; fears of being responsible for harming someone or something; and magical numbers, colors, images, or prayers that might cause harm or discomfort. Other types of ideas or images might also be obsessions if they come into mind repeatedly and are unwanted. The wide variety and sometimes unusual types of obsessions can make OCD difficult to identify. Also, because some types of intrusive ideas seem like obsessions but are not, it's important to consult a mental health professional familiar with this disorder who can make a careful diagnosis.

Compulsions or rituals are repeated behaviors or mental actions that are used to reduce anxiety or discomfort caused by an obsession. The goal in doing a ritual is to undo or "neutralize" the obsession. Most people recognize that these rituals are excessive but still feel compelled to do them in a particular way according to their own rules. Common compulsions include hand washing, showering, bathing, tooth brushing and grooming, cleaning household items, touching certain objects, checking drawers, locks, and appliances, and going back and forth through a door or repeating an action to undo a thought or image, placing things in a certain order, collecting and saving items so that nothing of value will be lost, having to do something exceedingly slowly to feel that it has been done properly, and seeking reassurance that something has or has not happened. Many people with OCD also have mental rituals like praying, repeating phrases in their mind, mental list making, substituting a good thought for a bad one, or taking back a bad thought. Just as obsessions vary in their frequency and intensity, compulsions may occur only rarely or consume many hours each day. Compulsive behaviors do not provide pleasure (like gambling or smoking or drinking alcohol); OCD sufferers do them to reduce tension, discomfort, or anxiety associated with obsessions.

Most people with OCD also avoid a variety of situations that they consider likely to provoke obsessions or rituals. Examples for someone with fears of contamination by dirt and germs are avoiding public rest rooms or shaking hands. Avoiding the stove and other appliances would be common for someone with fears of causing harm and with checking rituals. Although most people clearly recognize that their fears are irrational, this attitude is often hard to maintain when the person is in the middle of an obsession and feels highly anxious or very guilty.

What Else Is Known About OCD?

OCD was once thought to be relatively rare in the population, but recent community studies show that mild forms of the disorder may be relatively common. It is now estimated that about 2 percent of the population (one in fifty people) suffers from OCD. Childhood onset of OCD is common, but childhood symptoms often disappear and may reappear in a different form during adolescence and young adulthood. For women, the average age of onset is in late teens and early twenties and for men, it begins in early to middle teenage years. Men and women are affected almost equally, but slightly more women seek treatment. Most people with OCD wait an average of ten or more years after symptoms begin before seeking treatment. However, as information about psychiatric conditions has become more available and less stigma is associated with receiving psychological therapy, OCD sufferers are seeking treatment earlier.

OCD is typically a chronic condition that may wax and wane over time. The sufferer may go to great pains to hide the problem so that the disorder goes unnoticed, even by family members. However, when symptoms substantially impair a person's social, occupational, and family functioning, OCD is very difficult to hide. In some cases, compulsions may become the major life activity.

Many people with OCD also have another type of problem, such as depression, other anxiety disorders like social phobia and panic disorder, or Tourette's syndrome in which the person experiences uncontrollable motor or verbal tics. When depressed mood and feelings of hopelessness are very severe, depression may require treatment before treatment for the OCD begins. Some OCD clients also suffer from panic attacks in situations that trigger their obsessive fears. These are brief periods of high anxiety and associated physical symptoms, like heart racing, shortness of breath and dizziness, that are upsetting and can seem catastrophic at the time. If these panic symptoms in obsessive situations are especially troublesome, the person may need help learning to control panic before beginning treatment for obsessions and compulsions. Likewise, conditions such as Tourette's syndrome will require additional interventions, usually medications, prior to or at the same time as treatment for OCD. Some people with OCD who are overly sensitive to sensory experiences and tend to avoid social contact and have unusual beliefs or perceptual experiences or suspicious ideas may benefit from specialized behavioral treatments provided in settings that help reduce feelings of being emotionally overwhelmed. These kinds of additional treatments should be discussed with a therapist.

How Does OCD Begin?

Researchers have demonstrated that 85 to 90 percent of people have intrusive thoughts that are similar to those experienced by people with OCD. Obsessions are merely exaggerated versions of these normal mental intrusions. In fact, normal intrusive experiences are quite similar in their nature and content to those of OCD sufferers. This is clear from the types of mental intrusions reported by a group of ordinary people in the list below. Why do some people go on to develop OCD while others do not? One important difference between people who develop OCD and those who don't is how they react to the intrusive thoughts. People who don't develop OCD tend to realize that, although their intrusive thoughts are odd or unexpected, they don't have any special significance or meaning. Because of this, the intrusions don't disturb the person very much, and they occur less frequently and are easier to dismiss.

Obsessions Reported by a Nonclinical Sample

Impulse to hurt or harm someone

Thought of intense anger toward someone, related to a past experience

Thought of accident occurring to a loved one

Impulse to say something nasty and damning to someone

Thought of harm to, or death of, close friend or family member

Thought of acts of violence in sex

Thought that something is wrong with her health

Impulse to physically and verbally attack someone

Thought of harm befalling her children, especially accidents

Thought that probability of air crash accident to herself would be minimized if a relative had such an accident

Thought whether an accident had occurred to a loved one

Thought that she, her husband, and her baby (due) would be greatly harmed because of exposure to asbestos, with conviction that there are tiny asbestos dust particles in the house

Thought whether any harm has come to his wife

Impulse to shout at and abuse someone

Impulse to harm or be violent toward children, especially smaller ones

Impulse to crash car when driving

Impulse to attack and violently punish someone—e.g., to throw a child out of a bus

Impulse to say rude things to people

Thought about accidents or mishaps, usually when about to travel

Impulse to push people away and off, in a crowd—e.g., a queue

Impulse to attack certain persons

Impulse to say inappropriate things—"wrong things in the wrong place"

Impulse—sexual impulse toward attractive females, known and unknown

Thought—wishing and imagining that someone close to her was hurt or harmed

Thought of experiences many years ago when he was embarrassed, was humiliated, or was a failure

Impulse to violently attack and kill someone

Thought that she might do something dramatic like trying to rob a bank

Impulse to jump from top of a tall building or mountain/cliff

Impulse to sexually assault a female, known or unknown

Impulse to say rude and unacceptable things

Impulse to engage in certain sexual practices that involve pain to the partner

Impulse to jump off the platform when a train is arriving

Thought of physically punishing a loved one

Adapted from Rachman and DeSilva (1978). Copyright 1978 by Pergamon Press, Ltd. Adapted by permission.

In contrast, people who develop OCD tend to respond to these intrusive thoughts as if they represent real threats and need to be taken seriously. They try not to think about the thoughts that bother them, but unfortunately, this has exactly the opposite effect. That is, efforts to suppress thoughts actually increase their frequency. In addition, those who are fearful of the intrusive ideas begin to avoid situations that might provoke the thoughts. This often doesn't work, so the person tries to undo or neutralize them using behavioral or mental rituals. Unfortunately, avoidance and compulsive behaviors prevent the person from experiencing their thoughts fully and becoming used to them so that obsessions no longer provoke discomfort. In this way, obsessions and compulsions become quite entrenched, and the sufferer never has an opportunity to learn that simply tolerating the obsessions without avoiding or ritualizing eventually leads to reduction in the obsessive fears.

Biological factors undoubtedly play a role in the development of OCD. People with OCD appear to differ in their brain structure and chemistry compared to those without this disorder. It also seems likely that OCD can be transmitted genetically, since the disorder occurs more often among identical than fraternal twins, and the rate of OCD symptoms among immediate family members is higher than would be expected by chance. More information about biological factors can be found in the suggested readings at the end of this manual.

OCD might be more likely to develop in people who hold certain types of strong beliefs or assumptions that they learned previously in their families through religious or cultural training, or from other personal experiences. Sometimes, early experiences with rigid teachings make people more vulnerable to some of the beliefs and attitudes described below. Many of the types of obsessions that people with OCD have are focused on "gray areas" in which some element of normal risk is present for everyone. However, individuals with OCD often err on the side of excessive caution and tend to overestimate the likelihood of harm in comparison to others. Sometimes, it seems that people with OCD assume that a situation is dangerous unless it is proven safe. Of course, guarantees of safety are nearly impossible to prove, because there is always the possibility of error. Because they overestimate threat, OCD sufferers often have difficulty tolerating ambiguous situations, and worry whether their decisions and actions are right. They may also underestimate their ability to cope with these kinds of potentially dangerous situations.

Another problem with beliefs is that OCD sufferers attach too much importance to particular kinds of thoughts, mistakenly thinking that normal people don't have these thoughts. They may also have a magical idea that simply having a thought or an urge to do something increases the chances that it will actually come true. Of course, if someone thinks that intrusive thoughts are very important and could lead to harm, they are also likely to think that it is necessary to control their thoughts and actions. Many people with OCD also assume too much responsibility for a variety of situations. They are often as concerned about failing to prevent a problem as about causing one, and they tend to think that the responsibility for harm is theirs alone, rather than shared with others. Assuming responsibility for so many situations produces guilt, and it is not surprising that compulsions are used to relieve this guilt. Finally, some people with OCD are also quite perfectionistic—they think they should try to find the right solution to every problem and they worry that even minor mistakes will have serious consequences.

What Is the Effect of OCD on Families?

OCD can have unfortunate effects on the quality of family life and on family communication. Over time, many family members begin to actually participate in rituals and they may avoid situations at the sufferer's request. Often, family members are asked to provide frequent reassurance about obsessive fears. It is not very surprising that many family members become quite distressed and feel some responsibility for their afflicted relative's difficulties. Some become frustrated, and are critical or even hostile toward the OCD sufferer, while others, especially parents, become overly involved and even take over chores and duties that would normally be the OCD person's responsibility around the home. These reactions are all understandable, given the difficulty that OCD imposes on the sufferer and on family members. It is often helpful to involve family members in treatment, at least at some times, to enable them to have an opportunity to ask questions and decide what to do in difficult situations that can be upsetting for everyone.

Treatment of OCD

Over the past twenty-five years the prognosis for OCD has improved greatly. At present, about 70 percent of people with OCD improve with available treatments. The most significant symptom relief comes from behavior therapy, cognitive therapy, and medications that affect the body's serotonin system. Two main types of psychological therapy are very helpful for OCD: behavior therapy and cognitive therapy. These are described briefly below and are taught in detail in this manual. Information about medications is available in the suggested readings at the end of this manual or from a psychiatrist experienced in treating OCD.

Essential Components of Behavioral Treatment

An important goal of behavioral therapy is to disconnect obsessive thoughts, images, and impulses from the unpleasant fear and discomfort that they provoke. This is accomplished by exposure to situations that cause obsessions, so that the discomfort can gradually decrease. At the same time, the OCD sufferer must stop his or her rituals during the exposure and also stop avoiding situations that cause discomfort. Thus, the basic elements of behavioral treatment for OCD are:

- Exposure to feared obsessive situations

and

- Prevention of rituals and avoidance behaviors

These two parts of the treatment are applied simultaneously and gradually, depending on the person's tolerance for discomfort. This manual focuses on applying exposure gradually using a list of feared situations that is carefully planned in advance with a therapist. This treatment has been used in many research studies with excellent results.

During therapy sessions the therapist describes and often demonstrates how to do the exposures to make sure the sufferer is not avoiding obsessive situations. During this process, the therapist asks about discomfort levels regularly to ensure that the situation is manageable and a good choice for treatment. Exposure periods may last forty-five to ninety minutes and should result in a noticeable amount of improvement in discomfort. Each session usually begins with the previous exposure item and then progresses to new ones that are a little more difficult. Later sessions proceed in the same way, until all of the obsessive situations are confronted and anxiety is considerably reduced. It is rare for discomfort to disappear altogether, but most people notice considerable benefit that improves with time. In some cases it is helpful to do some exposures in imagination. In this case, the client and therapist plan imaginary scenes about the feared obsessions, and the therapist narrates parts of the scene while the client closes his or her eyes and imagines it in detail during treatment sessions. Just as for actual exposure, the sufferer is asked to keep imagining the scene until discomfort reduces noticeably. Loop tapes can facilitate exposure to some kinds of obsessions. With the help of the therapist, the client narrates the obsession onto a tape and replays this over and over.

During and after each exposure session, the OCD sufferer is asked not to engage in any rituals or avoidances that might interrupt or undo the exposure experience. This is done gradually, so that no compulsions are allowed in connection with exposures that are the focus of treatment in that week or from previous weeks. The client is asked to minimize any rituals that occur in situations that have not yet been included in the exposure treatment. Regular homework assignments are given after every session, and usually these are very similar to what was done during the treatment visit. If it makes sense to the client and the therapist, a family member might be asked to help during some homework assignments. Records should be kept of all homework assignments and of how the sufferer felt during the process. This enables the therapist to monitor progress and help with any problems.

Essential Components of Cognitive Therapy

We know that exposure and prevention of rituals by itself changes some irrational attitudes and beliefs about OCD symptoms. For example, most people begin to think differently about the likelihood of danger and their ability to tolerate anxiety and cope with intrusive experiences. Some may also change their attitude toward intrusive experiences so that these no longer seem so odd or bothersome, and they stop trying to control them. But these and other types of problematic thoughts may not change enough to enable the sufferer to make the best progress or to maintain their gains after treatment ends. Because of this, the therapist may recommend cognitive therapy in addition to behavioral treatment. In cognitive therapy, the therapist helps sufferers examine their interpretations and beliefs to develop an alternative way to think about the intrusive experiences that is much less threatening. Several specialized cognitive therapy techniques can be useful in this process. Although this therapy is relatively new, some published research suggests that individual cognitive therapy with a skilled therapist is as effective as behavioral treatment. The essential components of cognitive therapy are:

- Identification of irrational beliefs and attitudes

- Questions to examine the logic of interpretations and beliefs

- Specialized techniques to help challenge beliefs and attitudes

First, the therapist helps the client identify unreasonable interpretations and attitudes toward obsessive thoughts by repeatedly asking what the sufferer was thinking in an obsessive situation and what this means to them. For example, the therapist might ask, "So if that happened, what would it mean to you?" Also, the therapist asks clients to keep daily records of their thoughts to help them notice their thinking in various situations. Once the sufferer and the therapist understand what beliefs and attitudes commonly occur in obsessive situations, the therapist asks questions about the logic of the client's explanation of his or her thinking. Sometimes, the therapist may play the role of devil's advocate to help the client think clearly about the obsessions. The client is asked to think like a scientist in evaluating his or her own logic and the evidence for it and to conduct behavioral experiments to test predictions related to obsessive ideas. These experiments are often assigned as part of the exposures in behavioral treatment.

Several additional techniques are also taught to help challenge interpretations and beliefs that the client thinks might be irrational. Examples of these are:

- Learning to think about the entire range of an idea rather than just one small part of it

- Experimenting with the effects of trying to control obsessive thoughts compared to the effects of not interfering with these thoughts

- Calculating the real probability of all of the steps required for the obsessive fear of harm to actually occur

- Estimating all components of responsibility for a feared event, not just one's own

- Thinking about an obsessive fear from different perspectives, especially that of a judge or jury that has to evaluate the evidence

- Examining the advantages and the disadvantages of holding different views of an obsessive situation

Research Findings That Guide Treatment

Benefit from Exposure and Prevention of Rituals

More than twenty-five research studies have demonstrated that behavioral treatment reduces obsessions and compulsions. The benefits from this treatment persisted up to six years after treatment ended. Approximately 75 to 80 percent of clients can expect to benefit, and the majority of them are usually considered very much improved. Although most clients maintain their gains, some clients require additional treatment after the behavior therapy for OCD ends. Studies of serotonin reuptake inhibitor (SRI) medications such as clomipramine, fluoxetine, fluvoxamine, sertraline, and paroxetine have indicated that these medications by themselves partly reduce OCD symptoms for most OCD sufferers, but the amount of benefit may be slightly less than for behavior therapy. Adding these medications to behavioral treatment produces little additional benefit on average, but some sufferers find combined treatment quite helpful. Research has shown that the addition of special relapse prevention sessions to behavior therapy especially helps maintain improvement. These sessions help clients recognize potential obsessive problems and use coping skills to reduce anxiety after stressful experiences.

Benefit from Cognitive Therapy

Only a few studies have investigated the effectiveness of cognitive therapy for OCD symptoms. These studies show that cognitive treatment was quite effective by itself, even without behavioral therapy or medications. The most recent of these studies tested methods of cognitive therapy very similar to the ones included in this manual. In one of these studies, cognitive therapy produced excellent results that were slightly better than the benefits from behavioral treatment. Another study combined cognitive and behavioral treatments for clients who had obsessions and mainly mental rituals, which have previously been considered very hard to treat. The combined cognitive and behavioral treatment produced an 84 percent success rate and therapeutic gains were maintained one year later. Therefore, research indicates that cognitive therapy can be quite helpful in reducing OCD symptoms. In this manual, cognitive methods are recommended as additions to exposure and ritual prevention.

Goals of Treatment

It is important to remember that the goal of treatment for clients with OCD is not to eliminate intrusive thoughts, images, or impulses, but rather to remove their sting. That is, if almost all ordinary people experience intrusions, then eliminating them is virtually impossible. A more reasonable goal is to reduce the frequency, discomfort, and rituals associated with intrusions, so that they are easier to dismiss as habitual meaningless thoughts and easier to cope with when they persist for more than a few minutes. Most people who are treated for OCD will notice a gradual and quite substantial reduction in the severity, frequency, and duration of OCD symptoms by the end of treatment, and many will continue to improve after treatment is over. Improvement in everyday functioning in areas such as work, social relationships, and family life often occurs more slowly.

Most people find that stress exacerbates bad habits. Likewise, OCD sufferers will be prone to OCD symptoms in times of crisis. Also, biological factors, such as hormonal fluctuations accompanying pregnancy and menopause, may trigger OCD symptoms. Because of this, the last few treatment sessions address how to manage stressors and prevent the return of OCD symptoms. In some cases, a person might need some booster sessions to resolve increases in obsessions and compulsions. Generally, most OCD sufferers will need to continue to use the tools they learn in therapy to help them maintain their gains. Some clients may also suffer from other conditions that require additional therapy after the OCD treatment is completed, or they may need assistance with employment or social problems if these have been affected by the OCD. Generally, we recommend that clients work on one problem at a time to obtain the most benefit from therapy.

The Format for Therapy Sessions

Most behavioral and cognitive treatments for OCD require from fifteen to twenty-five sessions. This manual is designed for a sixteen-session treatment, but you and your therapist will need to determine together whether you need more or fewer sessions, depending on your response as treatment progresses. To design and carry out an effective behavioral and cognitive therapy for OCD, the therapist first collects detailed information about the client's symptoms. Usually, the therapist will interview the client and his or her family members and ask the client to complete several questionnaires and to keep records of obsessive fears and compulsive behaviors. In the first few interviews, the therapist will make a diagnosis, identify the specific symptoms of OCD, and obtain information about historical and current features and effects of the disorder, about previous treatment, and about any other problems or resources that might be important in recovery from OCD. Usually, one or more family interviews will also be scheduled to learn about how family members may be involved in symptoms and their reactions to the OCD. The questionnaires and self-monitoring provide additional information about the nature and severity of OCD and related symptoms to guide the treatment plan.

Also, during the first few sessions of treatment, the client and family receive education about OCD and about the treatment methods. Then, the therapist and client design a hierarchy. This is a list of situations that provoke obsessions, arranged from least to most disturbing. As described earlier, exposure treatment begins with the least disturbing items and progresses to more difficult ones while the client gradually stops rituals associated with these situations. All of the exposures are planned ahead and carried out during and between sessions as part of the homework. After several sessions of exposure and prevention of rituals, the therapist may introduce cognitive therapy methods to help the client examine his or her reasoning when thinking about obsessive situations. As described earlier, several types of cognitive methods will be used to help clients examine their thoughts from different perspectives. Homework is an essential part of therapy. Without it, clients cannot improve and learn enough skills to overcome their symptoms. Several different types of homework may be assigned, including exposure and blocking rituals between sessions and also recording and deliberately challenging thinking about obsessive situations. Sometimes family members might be able to assist with some homework assignments, but this will be planned during the therapy sessions.

The therapist and client begin each session by reviewing the agenda for that day. This helps keep treatment on track, so that neither person becomes sidetracked onto other topics. For each treatment session the therapist reviews the homework and then moves on to working on the exposures and prevention of rituals scheduled for that session and to cognitive techniques that might be especially useful during exposure. After this, the therapist and client agree on the homework assignment and whether a family member should assist. Each session follows this general format, adjusting exposures and homework assignments to the client's progress.

Before treatment ends, one or more follow-up meetings should be scheduled to ensure that progress continues and any problems are resolved. The therapist will also assess the degree of improvement in OCD symptoms at the end of treatment. After treatment ends, the client should be alert to warning signs that may indicate the need for booster sessions. These signs are increased discomfort to old or new obsessive thoughts, increased avoidance, and mild recurrence of old rituals or the appearance of new compulsions. If this happens, clients should not become alarmed, since often only a few sessions are needed to resolve the problem.

Session 1

Getting Started

Treatment Goals and Motivation

The introduction to this manual indicated that the goal of treatment for OCD is not to eliminate intrusive obsessions, thoughts, images, and impulses, but to reduce their frequency and the discomfort that is associated with them. Also, treatment aims to reduce or eliminate rituals and avoidance of obsessive situations. Because a successful outcome of treatment requires significant effort from clients who come regularly to sessions and do their homework as best they can, it is very important to be sure that you are ready to work seriously toward these goals. Sometimes people are afraid of the treatment itself, afraid that they won't be able to tolerate or cope with the therapy requirements or the discomfort. If this is your only concern, rest assured that the therapist will help you plan a treatment that suits your needs. Although sometimes you will feel uncomfortable, it is extremely unlikely that you will not be able to do the tasks, and you will always have an important role in deciding what the assignments are. The therapist will encourage you and help you find a pace that is feasible for you.

But sometimes, OCD sufferers are ambivalent about treatment for other reasons. Some people come into treatment because their partner or another family member has pressured them into it. Unfortunately, a half-hearted effort because someone else insists will not produce enough change to make the effort worth the trouble. It's important to think ahead to how you are likely to feel if you are successful in therapy and OCD is no longer a significant problem for you. Do you have anything to lose if your symptoms improve a lot? Some things you might lose are money, a special role in your family, and protection from duties and responsibilities that might seem overwhelming. For example, some people with OCD have applied for and are receiving disability payments because of their symptoms. If OCD improves along with everyday functioning, these payments are likely to stop. Sometimes, people with OCD are treated specially by their family members who take over their jobs and responsibilities; if OCD improves, they might be expected to resume doing these chores. Also, sufferers are sometimes worried about their ability to function effectively in a work setting or in social situations; if OCD prevents this now, then improvement in these symptoms might mean having to face these other problems. This can be quite scary, especially since no one knows in advance how they will feel and whether they will be able to cope with fears and learn new skills to feel more competent. If you feel ambivalent about treatment, be sure to discuss this with your therapist honestly so that a wise decision can be made about how to proceed.

Discussing OCD Symptoms

Your therapist will spend most of this session and the next asking questions about topics that are very important to making decisions about what symptoms to treat and how to design the therapy. These topics include your obsessions, your compulsions, and any situations that you avoid entering because of your obsessive fears. For example, the therapist will ask what circumstances cause you to feel the need to do your rituals and ask you for recent examples. It is important to know whether you have mental rituals like praying, making lists in your mind, or thinking good thoughts to fix bad ones. It is also important to learn whether you ask questions or seek reassurance from other people or from experts. These are like rituals and require special intervention during therapy. The therapist will also ask what you think would happen if you didn't do your rituals, for example, disease, death, fire, killing someone, going crazy, going to jail, and so forth. Finally, you'll be asked about what kinds of situations or activities you avoid because of your OCD symptoms. This will take some thought since you are more likely to notice what you do rather than what you don't do.

The therapist will also ask you about the history of your OCD, when it first began and whether the symptoms have fluctuated or changed between then and now. Your ideas about why they began and persisted are also important. You'll be asked how much time you spend on the OCD problems and how much they interfere with your ability to function, as well as whether other family members have had OCD or similar problems. Some people have other problems besides OCD, such as other anxiety conditions like the tendency to worry a lot, social fears or panic attacks, or other types of problems like eating disorders, problems with tics or impulsive behaviors, or problems with depression, alcohol or drugs, and so forth. Please be honest about these, since the therapist may have to adjust treatment to take these problems into account.

The therapist will want to know what other treatments you have tried for OCD, especially medications and whether you are taking any now and what effect they have had. It is not necessary to take medications to benefit from the treatment described in this manual. However, your therapist will advise you whether the addition of medications might be helpful in your particular case. If you are already taking medications, therapists generally prefer that you keep these stable during the behavioral and cognitive treatment so that it is clear what effect the psychological treatment is having. If you were to change your medications substantially during therapy, it would be difficult to figure out whether you were getting better because of the psychological treatment or the medication.

Asking Questions

Feel free to ask questions about your therapist's impression of your symptoms and whether they will respond to treatment. The vast majority of people with OCD can be treated with the methods that you will learn in this manual, but if you have concerns, it's important to raise these and ask for information so you can be sure this is the right treatment for you at this time. If you are living with your family, your therapist may also ask you to think about the possibility of inviting the family member(s) to attend some or all of the next session or two. Often family members can be very helpful in giving information you might not have thought about, and they may have a different perspective on your situation that the therapist may find important to understand.

Homework

Your therapist will probably ask you to fill out some questionnaires or forms that inquire about your OCD symptoms and other symptoms as well. Please be honest in your answers, but you do not need to be careful to get the "right" answer. Try hard not to be perfectionistic about completing these. Your first impressions are more important. You might also be asked at the end of this session or the next one to keep a record of your main obsessions and compulsions for several days. This helps the therapist understand when these symptoms occur and exactly what it feels like to you. To do this, you will learn to rate your discomfort level on a scale from 0 to 100 where 0 means very relaxed or no discomfort at all and 100 is the worst anxiety or discomfort you have ever felt in your life. We call this scale Subjective Units of Discomfort or SUDs. A form for keeping a record is included on the next page.

Self-Monitoring Form

Please record the actual *number of minutes* or *number of times* you perform rituals specified on this form. Please note the situation that led to your need to do the ritual, as well as the amount of discomfort on a scale from 0 to 100, where 0 means completely calm and 100 means extremely upset or disturbed.

Please note the following suggestions from your therapist for keeping records of rituals:

_____

_____

_____

_____

Example:

Ritual A: <u>Washing</u>   Ritual B: <u>Checking for harm</u>

Time of Day	Situation that led to ritual	Discomfort	Minutes Ritualizing	
			Ritual A	Ritual B
9:30 a.m	Took out the garbage	70	4 min.	
11:30 a.m.	Bathroom—urination	80	5 min.	
1:00 p.m.	Drove car to town center	85		10 min.
4:00 p.m.	Used iron	60		2 min.
6:30 p.m.	Cleaning up after dinner—stove, oven, faucet	55		15 min.

Continued on Next Page

Please record your ritual behaviors below:

Time of Day	Situation that led to ritual	Discomfort	Minutes Ritualizing	
			Ritual A	Ritual B

Session 2

Completing the Assessment

Review and Agenda Setting

Your therapist will usually being each session with a brief summary of what you worked on during the last session and the plan for this session. If you have any questions or comments, always feel free to voice these at the beginning of the time.

General History

Most of this session will be devoted to learning about your general history, including what it was like to grow up in your family, your social life as a child and an adult, your religious background, how you did in school, your past and present work situation, and your current family life. If you had any especially traumatic experiences, it is important to report these so the therapist understands what effect these might have had on you. These questions are designed to help the therapist understand your upbringing and experiences and how these might have influenced your OCD symptoms and affected your attitudes about various situations. You will also be asked about how your family has reacted to your OCD symptoms and about their views on why this problem developed. In particular, the therapist needs to know how your family accommodates to or is involved in your symptoms and how they feel about this. It is also important to learn how supportive your family members are and whether you get along so that they might be helpful during the treatment process.

Symptom Severity

After getting your history, the therapist will want to review your OCD symptoms in detail, especially to learn about any symptoms that didn't come up during the first session. You and your therapist will need to decide which symptoms should be the targets of the treatment and agree on the order in which they should be treated, if you have more than one obsession or compulsion. The therapist will look over your self-monitoring forms to understand how these symptoms occur on a daily basis, especially how much time they take and what triggers them. Sometimes, people have difficulty figuring out how to use these forms for record keeping. If this was true for you, your therapist will probably give new instructions that should work better for you. Your therapist may also ask questions to get a clear picture of the severity of the OCD problem.

Homework

Your therapist may ask you to complete other forms during the week and especially to begin to make a complete list of most obsessive situations that trigger rituals. This will form the basis for the treatment plan in which you will be gradually exposed to your feared situations. In the next session, the items on the list can be arranged according to how difficult they are for you. For now, just make as complete a list as possible, usually with fifteen to twenty-five situations that provoke obsessive fears. A blank list is given at the end of this session to help you. If you have more than one type of obsessive fear, you can make out another list of obsessive situations for each one.

Often, the therapist will want to arrange a family session for the next visit to discuss family involvement in symptoms, reactions to OCD, and to educate family members about OCD and the behavioral and cognitive treatment methods that will be used with you. Generally, only adult family members living at home or in regular contact with you will be invited to attend, although you should tell the therapist if you want someone in particular to attend.

List of Obsessive Situations

Obsessive Theme _____

Triggers for Obsessions   **Discomfort**
(specific situations, objects, or thoughts   (0–100)
that provoke obsessive fears)

1.

2.

3.

4.

5.

6.

7.

8.

9.

10.

11.

12.

13.

14.

15.

Family Assessment, Education, and Treatment Planning

Family Assessment

You and your family members will be interviewed together during this session, so that your family has a chance to describe what they have noticed about your symptoms. If your parents are attending, they might be asked about when the symptoms began and why they thought this happened at that time. They may also be able to comment on any changes they have observed over time. The therapist will also want to know how they feel about these symptoms and whether they blame themselves, as many parents do. Your family members will also be asked whether they accommodate to the OCD and if so, how. For example, many family members provide reassurance, wait for the OCD sufferer who may be doing rituals, avoid going into situations that upset the sufferer, perform compulsions for the sufferer, and take over tasks that are difficult for them to do. Because these efforts often produce frustration, the therapist will ask about your family members' reactions to the accommodation.

It is also useful to know how family members think about their relationship with you and how well you communicate with each other. Knowing family members' attitudes toward the treatment program can also be important, especially if it might be helpful to include them in the treatment. If you find that family members are not very supportive, they probably won't be included much in the treatment process, but it is still important for them to learn about the treatment so that they know what is happening and do not interfere mistakenly with the treatment process.

Behavioral Models for OCD

An important part of this session is educating you and your family members about the relationship of obsessions to compulsions and how the behavioral treatment works in relation to this. The following description helps clarify this.

Treatments for OCD derive from observations that many people have made about the function that obsessions and compulsions serve. That is, obsessions provoke anxiety and other negative emotions like guilt. In contrast to obsessions, compulsions or rituals (these are different names for the same thing) reduce discomfort, even if only briefly. So obsessive thinking causes discomfort, and compulsive behaviors and mental rituals reduce it. Some obsessions begin when a traumatic experience or frightening information triggers strong fear in a person and then becomes associated with other reminders of this unpleasant experience. The fearful person begins to anticipate and avoid any reminders of the negative experience. Think about whether this is true in your own experience. If it is, your reaction may be a bit like thinking that you are about to be attacked by a ferocious animal without really knowing when or even whether the animal is on the loose or locked up. You become concerned whenever anything hints of the animal's presence, and your tension helps you to be ready to protect yourself. A lot of uncertainty is involved, and when it is difficult to predict harm, people usually try very hard to control it. Perhaps your own rituals are an effort to control what seems like unpredictable fear reactions.

Even very irrational fears can become quite persistent in this way. They become habits that occur automatically. Once a fear or obsession is established, people naturally try to reduce their discomfort. For many people, an effective method is simply to avoid the fearful situation in the first place or to escape from it. But when the fear is caused by internal thoughts or images rather than actual situations, it is impossible to avoid or escape because you can't just turn off your thinking, although lots of people try. So people with obsessive thoughts develop more active ways to undo or prevent the fear by engaging in compulsive behaviors or mental rituals. But why would somebody keep doing these rituals when they are so time consuming and upsetting? This is because the rituals at least reduce discomfort a little or for brief periods, and even a brief reduction of bad feelings makes a person feel slightly better. It also strongly increases the chances that they will repeat whatever made them feel better. Figure 3-1 shows a model for how this works.

Figure 3-1: Behavioral Model for OCD

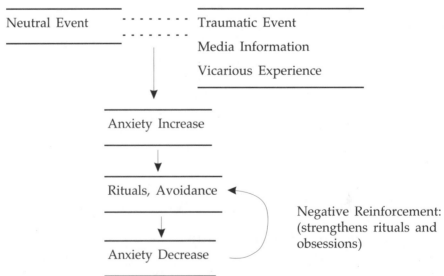

This is how people get caught in a vicious circle that doesn't seem to make a lot of sense unless you think about it carefully. The problem is that once people get hooked on compulsions to manage their obsessive discomfort, they never come into contact with their obsessive ideas or feared situations for long enough to get used to them. A good treatment for OCD, then, is exposure to feared situations and prevention of the rituals and avoidance that blocks this exposure. If people with OCD experience the things they fear for long enough, eventually they just get used to it. We call this "habituation" or "extinction" of emotional reactions. This is a lot like the experience we have when we first come into a room with a peculiar smell. After a while, we don't notice the smell; we just get used to it. Likewise, someone who lives near train tracks stops noticing when a train goes by, even though the sound is quite loud.

If compulsions or rituals interrupt the exposure, the anxiety reduction is also interrupted and discomfort stays high. So to be effective, exposure should not be interrupted with rituals, and these have to be stopped during exposures. To enable OCD sufferers to participate in treatment, you and your therapist begin with obsessions and situations that are less disturbing and work your way up to harder ones. This is why you need to develop a complete list of obsessive situations that can be arranged hierarchically from less to more discomfort. During therapy sessions, you'll actually go to those situations for exposure and also do this as homework. Sometimes, it is also helpful to use imagined exposures for certain types of symptoms that are hard to work on directly. For each exposure situation, you and your therapist will work on blocking all avoidance and rituals so that the exposure is prolonged enough to reduce discomfort. You'll be allowed to do some rituals in other situations that you haven't yet started working on. Eventually, you work your way through all of the obsessive situations and block all of the rituals. If you have any questions about this explanation for behavioral treatment, ask your therapist.

Much has been written about OCD as a biological problem. Research findings show that people with OCD do have biological features that are different from those without OCD. These include differences in the structure of the brain and in brain biochemistry. It is important that you understand that *both* serotonergic medications and behavioral treatments produce changes in the brain that cause OCD sufferers' brains to look more like those who don't have OCD. That means that there are several ways to correct OCD. One important advantage of behavioral treatment is that you will also learn skills that are useful in preventing a recurrence of obsessions and compulsions in the future. If you would like more information about biological features of OCD, you might want to read some chapters in the books on the reading list at the end of this manual, especially in the book by Jenike and colleagues (1998.)

Cognitive Models for OCD

People with OCD also seem to have certain kinds of mistaken interpretations about their obsessions and unhelpful attitudes that they've developed from experience. These types of thoughts might distort their view of some situations. For example, some people *think that just having certain kinds of thoughts is bad* and that they *need to control those thoughts* by not thinking them. The problem is that none of us can really control our thoughts in that way. In fact, researchers have demonstrated that trying to suppress obsessions actually strengthens them rather than reducing them. This happens because when people work hard not to think something, they become so vigilant about these unwanted thoughts that they are even more attuned to them than if they'd left them alone in the first place.

People with OCD also seem to *overestimate the threat* in various situations, when the real dangers are actually much lower. Because of this, they don't tolerate uncertainty well and often have to check over and over to make sure they haven't made important mistakes. Many people with OCD accept too much *responsibility* for situations and this leads to guilty feelings and rituals to undo the feared harm. Some people hold *perfectionistic or rigid attitudes*, perhaps because they were taught that it was important to "do it right." Often, however, it would be much better to accept some mistakes and get the job done. These kinds of general errors in thinking or beliefs usually can contribute greatly to obsessive thinking and lead to longer and more elaborate behavioral and mental compulsions.

Figure 3-2 shows a model for how cognitive features of OCD contribute to the problem of obsessions and rituals. The process begins with normal thoughts or images that approximately 90 percent of ordinary people have from time to time. A list of the kinds of thoughts people often have was given in the introduction to this manual. See if any of them are similar to your own obsessions. People interpret these intrusive thoughts to have a particular meaning. Interpretations are influenced by a person's mood and by other events that cause stress. Sometimes people interpret intrusions differently when they have heard or read something recently in the news; that is, information can affect what you think about an intrusive thought. When an interpretation is especially anxiety or guilt provoking, most people try to reduce their discomfort with avoidance or rituals, which only work temporarily.

Figure 3-2: Model of Cognition in OCD

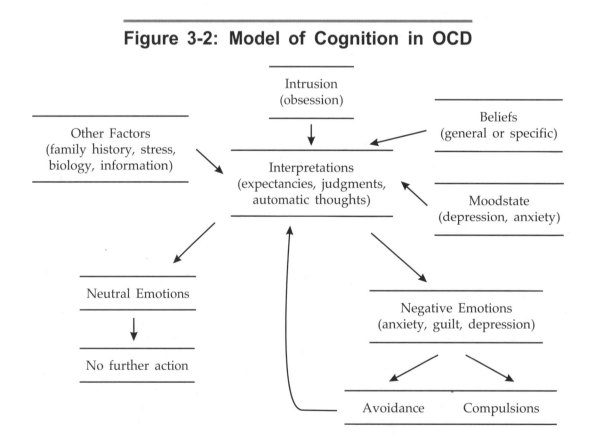

To correct some of the mistaken thinking that people with OCD might have, your therapist may use cognitive therapy techniques during the exposure treatment. Several techniques can help correct thinking errors and help speed up the recovery process. Still, it is easier to change behaviors like compulsions than it is to change the way people think. This takes longer but may be an important part of the therapy process. The treatment described in this manual begins with exposure and response prevention based on the behavioral model and gradually incorporates cognitive strategies based on the cognitive model. If you have any questions about the cognitive or exposure parts of the treatment, be sure to ask your therapist.

What your therapist will be trying to do in treatment is to make obsessive thoughts much less disturbing and help you to stop avoiding them or stop using rituals or any other undoing strategy to get rid of them. He or she will also help you to think differently in reaction to intrusive thoughts, so that they stay with you a short while, bother you only a little, and then gradually go away. Eventually, your obsessive thoughts will also become less frequent because they don't bother you much and don't produce the same intense urge to get rid of them. Instead, you just live with them for a bit until they go away.

Family Assistance with the Therapy

Inviting a family member to assist in treatment depends on whether you would find the assistance helpful. If you wish, discuss this with your therapist so you can work out a plan for the treatment sessions and for homework that will be feasible for both you and your relative. The therapist will also need to talk to your relative about how to assist in treatment. Usually, this mainly involves attending sessions occasionally so everyone has the same understanding of the treatment plan. Sometimes relatives will be asked to help with exposure homework assignments at home or in other settings. Also, your therapist will need to advise your relative how to respond in certain kinds of situations that can be confusing.

Homework

Your therapist will ask to see your list of obsessive situations and may request that you work on finalizing this list for next time. Your hierarchy is likely to be a main focus of the next session.

Session 4

Exposure and Response Prevention

Agenda

For this session you will need to decide whether you are ready to proceed with exposure treatment. This will include revising your hierarchy list and beginning the actual exposure, starting with the first item(s) on your list. Goals for this session will likely be to reduce your obsessive fears during exposure, to think about how to begin returning to more normal patterns of living, and to identify more appropriate ways to cope effectively with daily stressors. It is important for you to learn to become an expert in your own treatment, and therefore, the therapist will help you learn how to do the exposures and how to interrupt or prevent rituals when you have an urge to do these. Exposure treatment requires much effort and courage. It might be helpful for you and your therapist to draw up a written therapy contract like the one at the end of this session so that you are both very clear about your responsibilities and activities during treatment.

Developing the Hierarchy

You have already begun to make a list of situations that provoke your obsessive fears and rituals. Now it's time to review the list to be sure that it contains nearly all of the important obsessional situations that you are aware of. You may have more than one list because you have more than one type of obsessive fear. Examples of different hierarchy themes are contamination by pesticides, being dishonest, and causing harm by negligence. Don't be concerned if you have several types of fears. This is not likely to impede your treatment since each obsession can be treated in turn. Items on your list should be organized according to the degree of discomfort they provoke on the 0 to 100 SUDs scale described earlier. Examples of hierarchies from patients with different types of OCD symptoms are given below to give you an idea of what to include and how to organize yours. Of course, your list(s) will be quite different from these, matching your particular fears.

Fears of Dirt and Germ Contamination

Item	Discomfort	Session
Floor in therapist's office	40	1
Waiting room chairs	45	2
Door knobs in office and waiting area	50	2
Hallway floor	55	3
Door knob outside the bathroom door	55	3
Shopping mall benches	55	3
Office bathroom sink, soap dispenser	60	4
Office bathroom floor, inside doorknob	65	5
Shopping mall floor	65	5
Office bathroom toilet seat	70–75	6
Shopping mall bathroom sink counter, knobs	75	6
Shopping mall bathroom toilet seat, sanitary container	85	7
Using bathroom in shopping mall	90	8
Using bathroom in train or bus station	95	9

Fears of Harming Others

[kids in another room]

Item	Discomfort	Session
Sight of scissors on the table	30	1
Sight of paring knife on the counter	40	1
Sight of 6" kitchen knife on the counter	45	2
Using paring knife to cut vegetables	50	2
Using kitchen knife to cut vegetables	55	3
Sight of large knife	55	3
Using large knife	60	4

Item	Discomfort	Session
[kids sitting at kitchen table]		
Using paring knife	70	5
Using kitchen knife	75	5
Using large knife	80	6
[kids at sink or counter]		
Using paring knife	85	7
Using kitchen knife	90	7
Using large knife	100	8

AIDS fears

Item	Discomfort	Session
[at AIDS Action Center]		
Sitting in waiting area, handling literature	45	1
Using public rest rooms	50	1
[at Neighborhood Health Center]		
Sitting in waiting area for AIDS testing	50	2
Using public phones, doorknobs	55	2
Touching floors, trash can	65	3
Using public rest rooms	70	3
Going to restaurants and stores with probable gay waiters/salespeople	70	4
Using public facilities at these restaurants/stores	75	5
Sitting on benches in area frequented by possible drug users [safe times/places only]	80	6
[Hospital Emergency rooms]		
Sitting in waiting area	80	7
Using public rest rooms	90	7

Planning Exposures

Sometimes the exposures to your obsessive fears can be done in or near your therapist's office. For example, you might be able to bring many of your feared items into the office in a bag and then handle them while your therapist is present. Often, however, it will be necessary to do your exposures in your home, in your workplace, at shops or public places, or in other settings that you must travel to. It is often helpful to have your therapist go with you to these settings, especially the first time, but sometimes this may not be possible. Whatever your particular circumstance, planning the next several exposure sessions will require a careful review of the items on your hierarchy to determine how to implement the exposures and which ones should come first. Once you are confident that you can complete the exposure alone or with telephone assistance from your therapist, these situations can be assigned as homework. In any case, next to each hierarchy item should go the number of the session in which it will occur and the exact location of the exposure so that you and your therapist know what is planned for when.

If you have more than one type of obsession and ritual, it is usually best to begin with one of them and make some progress on that one before moving on to the next type of situation. Remember that for each exposure situation, you will also need to stop doing any rituals that you would normally do in that context. This takes quite a lot of courage, but most people can do this with the therapist's assistance.

Beginning Exposure and Response Prevention

To do the exposure to the first item on your hierarchy, you will need to make sure that full contact occurs. This means that if your fears are about contamination or things you don't like to touch, you should touch it completely without protecting any area of your body, clothes, purse, or other thing you usually try to keep clean. Touch the item(s) with the palms of your hands and especially your fingertips, then touch your hands to your face and hair and all parts of your clothing, handling things in your wallet or purse and so forth. Be sure not to avoid any part of the contact and don't do any rituals, even small ones like wiping or brushing off the contamination. Even brief little rituals interfere with getting used to the item and prolong the whole process. Your therapist will try to help you do this as fully as possible.

Your therapist will ask you about your discomfort level to see how you are reacting. Be sure to be honest in reporting this so that your therapist can make adjustments in the kind of exposure you do. It's important to feel some significant discomfort in order to learn to have a different response to the obsessive situation. Sometimes you might react with strong fear or other emotions; your therapist will help you manage your discomfort while you keep doing the exposure.

You will need to repeat the exposure or keep thinking about it to get the maximum benefit from the process. If you have checking rituals, you will probably be asked to do an activity without any checking and then keep the activity in mind. Depending on the nature of your symptoms, you may be advised to go on to other things or to keep ruminating about the first exposure without ritualizing. Your therapist will ask you about your emotional reaction every few minutes and will explore with you all aspects of your fears during the exposure. This means your thoughts, how you feel and how your body reacts, any catastrophic ideas that occur to you, memories, images, and so forth. This discussion helps you emotionally process your obsessive fears to the fullest extent. You should continue the exposure until you notice that some reduction in discomfort (called "habituation") occurs. Notice that when you stick it out, eventually you do feel better without any rituals or avoidance. If you run out of time before your discomfort decreases noticeably, your therapist might ask you to continue the exposure without rituals afterwards and to call in to report on the experience.

Response-Prevention Plan

It is very important to stop all rituals entirely during and after the exposure, including mental rituals, asking for reassurance or reassuring yourself in a compulsive way, and any other little compulsions you are tempted to do. By ritualizing you don't learn that if you just left the obsessional fears alone, eventually you would feel better without the ritual. That is, you learn the wrong lesson, thereby undoing the work of the exposure session. If you encounter situations during the week that you have not yet worked on as part of the exposure, you may be allowed to do a brief ritual but then you must repeat the exposure from today's session or from your homework. Otherwise, there is a significant danger that the ritual that you do in another context might undo some of the good exposure work you have already done. Generally, you and your therapist will use a gradual response-prevention plan with the following steps:

- Try to avoid exposure situations that are higher on your hierarchy whenever possible.

- Reduce all ritualizing to a minimum as agreed between you and your therapist.

- Stop all rituals and avoidance connected to current and previous exposure situations.

- Minimal rituals are allowed in difficult situations not yet encountered in treatment.

- Immediately following permissible rituals, re-expose yourself to the most recently practiced exposure items.

The overall goal is to maximize exposure and minimize ritualizing, while still enabling you to tolerate discomfort and gain confidence in your ability to make positive steps.

Homework

You will need to do exposure homework every day or nearly every day until your next session. These assignments will usually include situations similar to ones you worked on during the session, but in other contexts to facilitate generalization to other settings—especially ones you encounter frequently during the week. Sometimes, homework might also include other kinds of exposure situations because they provoke similar levels of discomfort as the ones in the treatment session. When you work on exposures by yourself, you might have a little more discomfort because a familiar and supportive person is not there. Often, a supportive family member is a good substitute. When your therapist assigns a homework task, be sure that you indicate whether you are confident that you can do it. If you are not, tell the therapist so both of you can figure out what assignment might be better. However, it is also important that you challenge yourself. You will not make good progress unless you are willing to try out exposures that are sometimes a bit difficult for you.

Record your homework assignment on a Homework Form that is provided at the end of this chapter. This form asks for a description of the exposure context, how long you worked on it, and whether you were able to stop rituals. You will need to complete one of these forms daily, so please make copies or get copies from your therapist.

Family Assistance

If a family member will be assisting you, you and your therapist should decide whether to invite him or her to attend all or part of the exposure session and homework planning. This enables your relative to observe how your therapist behaves during the exposure process. Generally, your family assistant will be mainly an observer, helping you by asking occasional questions or making supportive or informational comments. Your relative's role is to:

- Be available if possible when you need assistance or support during daily exposure homework

- Observe your progress during homework or other exposure situations

- Take note and report any observations that may be of interest to you and your therapist in planning treatment. This includes observation of avoidance and/or "mini-rituals" that you do that you might not have noticed.

Your relative should not provide reassurance that might serve the same purpose as a ritual. You and your relative should agree on the procedure for contacting your therapist by phone if there is any confusion between sessions about homework assignments.

Treatment Contract

1. We agree to meet according to the following schedule: _____
   _____
   [preferably twice weekly for four to six weeks and then weekly for approximately sixteen sessions]

2. We agree to attend all appointments, arriving on time and prepared for sessions.

3. We agree to jointly plan the agenda for behavioral therapy (and cognitive therapy if agreed upon).

4. We will select obsessive situations, thoughts, or objects for exposure based on a hierarchy we develop according to the degree of discomfort each context provokes.

5. I, _____, agree to engage in full exposure to agreed upon items until they provoke minimal discomfort and no rituals. We will proceed from easier to more difficult situations.

6. We agree to work to complete the most difficult exposure items approximately 75% of the way through treatment to allow repetitions of exposures that are still uncomfortable.

7. If some situations have been left out of the hierarchy by mistake, we will include these in exposures as treatment progresses.

8. I, _____, agree to stop all rituals after exposure to hierarchy situations. However, if I encounter obsessive situations not yet included in my assignments, I may complete minimal rituals if I immediately re-expose myself to items previously practiced during exposure.

9. If we determine that imagined exposure may be useful, some sessions will be devoted to this treatment.

10. I, _____, agree to complete all assigned homework on a daily or near daily basis and record my anxiety levels on an appropriate form.

11. If we determine that cognitive therapy may be useful, we will work to identify problematic interpretations of obsessive ideas and compulsive behaviors and to evaluate the validity of these interpretations.

12. We also agree to work to develop alternative thinking patterns to reduce obsessive and compulsive symptoms.

13. We will agree upon daily homework for cognitive treatment and will review the assigned homework for each session.

14. We agree to review progress toward therapy goals on a regular basis to help determine the next steps in treatment.

Continued on Next Page

15. We agree to jointly discuss and plan strategies to help maintain the benefits of this therapy.

16. We also agree to the following special plans: _____

   _____

   _____

Signature _____   Signature _____

Date _____   Date _____

Final List of Obsessive Situations

Obsessive Theme _____

Triggers	Expected Discomfort (0–100)	Session No.
1. _____	_____	_____
2. _____	_____	_____
3. _____	_____	_____
4. _____	_____	_____
5. _____	_____	_____
6. _____	_____	_____
7. _____	_____	_____
8. _____	_____	_____
9. _____	_____	_____
10. _____	_____	_____
11. _____	_____	_____
12. _____	_____	_____
13. _____	_____	_____
14. _____	_____	_____
15. _____	_____	_____

Homework Form

Name: _____ Date: _____

Week number:

Homework Exposure:

Time to Practice:

Anxiety levels:

Beginning:	40 minutes:
10 minutes:	50 minutes:
20 minutes:	60 minutes:
30 minutes:	

   Comments:

Homework Exposure:

Time to practice:

Anxiety levels:

Beginning:	40 minutes:
10 minutes:	50 minutes:
20 minutes:	60 minutes:
30 minutes:	

   Comments:

Session 5

Direct and Imagined Exposure and Response Prevention

Agenda

The agenda for this session includes a review of your homework and exposure to the next items on the hierarchy plus response prevention. In addition, you will learn how to do imagined exposure or loop tape exposures if these are needed in your case. Be aware that not all OCD sufferers will need to use these procedures for exposure to be effective.

Reviewing Homework

First, your therapist will review the homework assigned from last session to make sure that this experience was helpful. Some people may experience higher than expected anxiety during the homework. This means the exposure is activating obsessive fears, as it should. If you can tolerate the discomfort, anxiety eventually declines and you are likely to make good progress despite your discomfort. This takes more time for some people than for others. If you are having trouble completing your exposure homework or stopping your rituals as you had agreed, it is time for a discussion with your therapist about what is interfering with your progress. Remember that anytime you use rituals or avoidance to manage your anxiety during exposure homework, you are actually strengthening the OCD habits and making your own task more difficult.

Exposure

You and your therapist will select one or more items from your list for exposure for this session. You might notice some increase in discomfort compared to how you felt at the end of the last session. This is quite common. Usually anxiety rebounds a little between sessions and this is not a cause for concern. As before, observe your reactions carefully during the exposure process and report them to your therapist. Your therapist will ask you about your level of discomfort and help you engage fully in the exposure process. Try not to be tentative in doing the exposures, because this is a kind of avoidance designed to protect you. Instead you need to screw up your courage and take the plunge to see how you respond. If your family assistant is present, he or she might help you push yourself.

As soon as you can tolerate the exposure reasonably well, check with your therapist about adding the next item on the hierarchy. Sometimes you'll be able to include more than one hierarchy item in a single session, especially if both are conveniently accessible. However, you don't need to push yourself too hard if your discomfort level is still high. Follow your therapist's lead in the exposure, making sure that you do the exposure as completely as possible. Report your anxiety level when asked and focus on any obsessive ideas that occur to you. You can vary the exposure cues from time to time to encourage anxiety reduction in similar situations. Whenever you can, see if you can do the exposure yourself without help from your therapist. Between sessions, you'll want to be able to do homework assignments without an assistant or to handle exposure situations that occur unexpectedly during the day.

Sometimes during treatment, you will be asked to do things that most people do not ordinarily do unless they have to. Remember that most other people also don't have OCD and that they *could* do the exposure if the situation required it. To really get over a fear, it is very important to confront your worst fears and to become comfortable with the worst part of the problem, not just the easier parts. Complete exposure now decreases the chances that your OCD symptoms will return later on, after therapy has ended.

Imagined Exposure and Loop-Tape Methods

For some types of obsessions and compulsions, it may be very useful to replace direct exposure with imagined exposures or loop-tape exposures, at least for some sessions. These methods are described here.

In some cases, direct exposure to feared cues doesn't provoke all of the OCD sufferers' fears of disasters. In other cases, direct exposures are very difficult to implement with your therapist present. For these situations, your therapist might suggest a procedure called imagined exposure which has the same kinds of effects that direct exposure does. First, you and your therapist construct a series of scenes that can be arranged, beginning with easier ones and progressing over the next several sessions to more difficult ones. These are tape recorded during the office session for replay as homework assignments.

Together, you and your therapist outline a scenario in which you encounter the triggers for your obsessive discomfort. The scene usually includes one or more of your feared disastrous outcomes. Then, sit back in a comfortable chair with your eyes closed and listen to your therapist begin to describe the scene. Your therapist will ask you frequently for information about what you are seeing in the image using questions like: "What do you see now? Describe what's happening now. What do you hear [see, feel, smell, etc.]? What are you thinking? What is your reaction? How clear is the image on a scale from 0 to 100? Tell me your discomfort level on a scale of 0 to 100." These questions enable the therapist to be sure that you are imagining the scene clearly and experiencing it fully. Be sure to be honest in your reporting, especially if you are having a problem forming the image clearly. During the scene, be sure that you do not imagine doing rituals or avoiding the triggers for your obsessive fears. The scene will be taped so you can play it back later as homework.

Endless-Loop Tapes

If you have obsessions that are mainly accompanied by mental rituals, it may be especially helpful to record your obsession in your own voice onto a loop tape that plays over and over. This permits repeated exposure to the obsession without interruption from the mental ritual. Examples of obsessions that lend themselves to this procedure are blasphemous, vulgar, or "immoral" thoughts, bad words, or unlucky numbers that pop into your mind. These obsessions usually provoke neutralizing or "undoing" self-statements, prayers, or other thinking rituals. You or your therapist can buy a loop tape of the right length to match the typical duration of your obsessive intrusion (for example, one-, two-, or three-minute tape). You and your therapist should first decide on the best wording for your obsessive thoughts and you can then narrate one or more of these thoughts aloud onto the tape. Then, listen to this tape during the therapy session and pay attention to the words and their meaning without inserting any mental rituals that you usually use. The therapist will also ask you to listen to this tape as a homework assignment for long enough to produce some reduction in discomfort. If you have several different kinds of disturbing intrusions, you and your therapist can arrange these in a hierarchy for exposure in the next several sessions.

Family Assistance

If your family member attends this session, he or she will learn the best ways to be helpful at home to encourage you in following the treatment. Your relative can call the therapist in case of any confusion between sessions. All of you should also discuss ways in which your family accommodates to your OCD symptoms and whether some changes in these accommodating behaviors may be appropriate at this point. A goal of the treatment is to reduce family accommodation and this can be accomplished gradually as you make progress on your exposures.

Homework

You and your therapist can agree on homework assignments that match the level of exposure difficulty at which you have been working. Homework might include direct exposure and/or imaged or loop-tape exposures. Usually imagined or loop-tape exposures are assigned daily or near daily for about an hour a day. In the case of loop tapes, this may be broken into shorter periods, and in the case of imagined scenes, more time might be needed to reduce discomfort. Your therapist will give you specific instructions for you and/or your family member. Be sure to be alert for compulsive and avoidance behaviors so you can stop these during homework.

Session 6

Continuing Exposure and Response Prevention

Agenda

The agenda for this session includes reviewing your homework assignments, exposure to hierarchy items, and prevention of rituals, along with planning homework exposures and blocking compulsions, reassurance-seeking and avoidance, and discussion of family responses.

Reviewing Homework

You and your therapist will review homework from the previous session by examining the Homework Form and discussing any problems or difficulties. If you have any concerns, be sure to raise them at this time. Exposure, especially without the help of your therapist, requires quite a lot of courage.

Exposure

You and your therapist should proceed as planned to the next items on the hierarchy. Take the lead in doing the exposure as much as you can, even if you feel somewhat reluctant. Focus on the exposure and on obsessive concerns you have. Let your therapist know what level of discomfort you experience and discuss any thought processes that accompany the exposures. Look for other situations for exposure that are similarly difficult to encourage generalization of the learning process to other contexts. If your discomfort decreases fairly quickly to the hierarchy items, you can begin working on the next items. As always, be active in your contact with the exposure situation and focus on the experience and on any associated thoughts, images, emotional responses, and perceptions. Your therapist will ask for a report of your discomfort level every few minutes to check on your progress. If you are able to continue the exposure after the session, this may help you make even more progress.

Some people with fears of contamination feel the contact on their skin as a tingling sensation that transfers to other parts of their skin with direct touch and that may be especially difficult to tolerate because of the physical feelings. However, most physical sensations, even somewhat painful ones, lessen with time if you can just tolerate the discomfort for a while. You may find it helpful to experiment with what you notice about the exposure experience to see if you can decrease your sensitivity to the item. Sometimes, a person's attention can help or hinder the exposure process.

Sometimes what used to seem like minor OCD symptoms before you started treatment can become more prominent as you make progress on your hierarchy items. As anxiety reduces to the problem you are working on, old fears sometimes recur because now there is mental room to worry about these ideas again. This is a common experience for many OCD sufferers and is not a cause for alarm. It only means that you and your therapist need to develop another hierarchy and include exposures to the new fears. These are just as likely to habituate as the ones you've already worked on, often more rapidly than the original ones, and eventually you will "run out" of obsessions.

Imagined and Loop-Tape Exposures

If you have also been working on exposure to imagery scenes or to a loop-tape narration, you and your therapist can add new components to the scenes or tapes from the next step on your hierarchy. Generally, it is wise to avoid beginning a new scene of greater difficulty unless you have enough time remaining in the session to enable you to become accustomed to the images. The format for taped exposures will be similar to the previous ones.

Response Prevention

Sometimes OCD sufferers have difficulty distinguishing between reasonable coping strategies during exposure and ritualistic ones that should be prevented. Most of the time, if you just ask yourself whether it "feels like a ritual," you'll be able to tell whether your responses to the obsessive anxiety should be continued or blocked. Rituals have a driven quality to them so the person needs to repeat the effort or do it correctly in a particular and often stereotypic fashion. In contrast, coping responses simply help a person feel a little more comfortable by thinking in a more rational way. If you notice that you have begun to develop a new ritual, don't be alarmed, but be sure to discuss this with your therapist so you can figure out how to block it effectively.

Likewise, be observant of your need to obtain reassurance, since this often serves the same purpose as a ritual. Reassurance reduces discomfort but does not assist you in finding your own way to calm yourself in the face of obsessions. Of course, you have every right to ask for information when you do not know the answer to a question. However, if you find that the answers do not satisfy you or that you want to ask the same question again to be sure you heard it right and to calm your anxiety, consider this to be a ritual. Similarly, you may be tempted sometimes to try to assign responsibility for a situation to your therapist or to a family member rather than making your own decision about possible harmful outcomes. Again, try to resist this urge and discuss the problem with your therapist.

Family Assistance

Some people have difficulties with family members and may need help learning how to problem-solve to resolve these. If problems in negotiating planned exposures and blocking avoidance and rituals arise between you and your relative(s), you and you therapist may wish to consider a process called behavioral contracting. This usually involves an exchange of agreements in which each of you expresses a goal and agrees on how it should be implemented. First, your therapist helps you and your relative(s) focus on and define a problem. Then, each of you alternates making suggestions of possible ways to correct the problem. After some discussion of the possible advantages and disadvantages of the suggestions, your therapist will encourage agreement on a homework contract that specifies who will do what and when. Your family may need to rehearse how each of you will respond; for example, how your relative would remind you or what to say when expectations are met or not met. Depending on the outcome of the family contract between sessions, your therapist may need to help you renegotiate the plan.

Homework

You and your therapist need to agree on the daily homework for this week, depending on progress during today's session. Try to select several items in different settings to promote generalization of your gains to as many other situations as possible. Consider in advance whether you think you might have difficulty resisting rituals or avoidance behaviors and discuss these concerns with your therapist to work out a plan.

Exposure and Beginning Cognitive Therapy

Agenda

The agenda for this session includes review of your homework and continued exposure to items on the hierarchy. Your therapist may also include cognitive therapy during exposure if this seems reasonable at this time.

Homework Review

As always, it is important to review your exposure homework to be sure that adequate time was spent on exposure and you were able to control your rituals. If you are having any problems with homework, be sure to discuss these so that you and your therapist can decide what to do. Also, if you are having any problems with family communication about OCD symptoms, discuss this with your therapist.

Exposure and Ritual Prevention

The session will begin with exposure to the previous and/or next item on your hierarchy, depending on your homework experience and whether you are becoming more comfortable with obsessive situations worked on so far. At this point you are probably able to practice exposure by yourself fully without being told what to do. If you haven't already done so, it is important that you begin to practice exposure without your therapist having to direct you as much as before. Be sure that you fully attend to the fear cues by thinking about your thoughts and emotions during the exposure. Notice your discomfort level and report this to your therapist, along with how strongly you feel the urge to do a ritual. If your anxiety reduces quickly, it might be wise to move to another similar situation to be sure that you get used to different situations of the same type. This ensures that you learn to adapt to a variety of feared situations besides the first one you try.

If you have been working on imagined exposure scenes or loop tapes of your obsessive thoughts, proceed as before and increase the level of difficulty of the scene or tape to match your progress so far.

Cognitive Therapy

You and your therapist have probably already talked about some of your interpretations about the meaning of your obsessive thoughts when these actually occur and some of the assumptions or beliefs that you have about your feared ideas. Your therapist will probably write these down from time to time, and will discuss them with you. You might want to pay attention to statements that you make that use words like "always," "never," and "constantly." These words usually signal some exaggeration of reality, since very few situations can be accurately described in these kinds of absolute terms. Some examples of OCD sufferers' interpretations of intrusions and of beliefs are listed below to help you notice your own thoughts of this type.

Interpretations of Intrusions

- Whenever I have these thoughts, I feel like I'm losing control.

- I'm afraid that the fact that I have this thought means I'm going to act on it.

- The more I think about these things, the greater the risk they will come true.

- If I ignored these thoughts and something really happened, I couldn't stop blaming myself.

Beliefs/Assumptions

- I believe I could really hurt someone.

- Ordinary people don't get the kind of weird thoughts I do.

- You never know when you're going to regret something.

- I just think I shouldn't take the risk.

- If I don't fix the problem when I see it, somebody will get hurt.

- In a way, I'm responsible just because I knew about it.

- I just can't stand it when I don't know the answer.

- My father was right—when you can't do it right, you shouldn't do it at all.

This is a good time to look back at the introduction and session 3, where the cognitive model of OCD was explained. This model presumes that your obsessions have become a problem, at least in part because of how you interpret the intrusive obsessions when they occur. Instead of just being surprising but not especially alarming ideas, they've become fearful ones. Remember to think of how the thoughts affect your emotions and also your behaviors. At the end of this session, we've drawn a diagram called the Cognitive Triangle to show the influence of thoughts, feelings, and behaviors on each other. Discuss with your therapist how this applies specifically to your intrusive thoughts that contribute to your obsessions and compulsions. By now, the interpretations that are linked to your obsessions have become thinking habits that are so routine you have probably stopped questioning them. You probably also have some basic assumptions and beliefs that are also so automatic that you are hardly aware of them; usually you've often grown up thinking these ideas were correct.

Your therapist will help you figure out what these intrusions and beliefs are so that you can examine them more closely to see whether they should be changed. Your therapist will help you do this by using what we call the scientific method. This means that you and your therapist will consider each idea carefully to see if there is good evidence to support your beliefs and interpretations or whether there are alternative ideas that might actually be more likely or have more supporting evidence. To use this method, your therapist will ask you questions about your thoughts and rephrase what you say to be sure you both understand clearly what you think and why you think it. This helps you explore the logic that you use to support or refute your beliefs. Often, this can be done very effectively during exposures because this is when the ideas associated with your obsessive thinking come to mind most readily. As you and your therapist discuss your ideas, be on the lookout for conclusions that you have drawn that seem illogical when you look at them closely, but yet you believe them when you have an intrusive thought. Your therapist will probably have some ideas for how to help you examine them closely and how to change them if you decide they really don't make sense to you anymore.

One strategy for helping you begin this process is to determine your worst case scenario for your obsessive ideas to see what your most basic fear is about. This can usually be identified through a process called downward arrow in which your therapist repeats questions like: "So if that happened, what would that mean?" "And if that happened, what would/could happen next?" "If that occurred, why would that be so bad?" Eventually, you reach a "bottom line" and can think of no worse consequence of this sequence of events. Examples of ultimate fears are being rejected by someone important to you, dying, being a bad mother, being responsible for someone's death, going to hell, being humiliated or finding out you are stupid. To help you use this method, a Downward Arrow Form is included at the end. Two examples of the beliefs of OCD sufferers are given below:

Example 1

I will write an incorrect bank account number, and
the money will go to the wrong person.

↓

I will never get my money back.

↓

I will be responsible for the error and I will lose my
legal right to get my money back.

↓

I will live in poverty for the rest of my life.

Example 2

If I let my daughter's friend come over to play,
she might touch the woodwork in our old house.

↓

She'll eat the paint and get lead poisoning.

↓

Her parents will blame me for letting her come near the paint.

↓

I'll be an irresponsible parent.

↓

Other people will never let their children play with my daughter.

↓

My daughter will be rejected socially and it will be my fault.

↓

I won't be able to live with myself.

It is also important to figure out what the main themes of your intrusive thoughts and beliefs are. These are likely to fall into several categories that seem to be common for people with OCD. These themes are overestimating threat, intolerance for ambiguity, overestimating the importance of your thoughts and your need to control them, accepting excessive responsibility for events, holding perfectionistic standards for your behavior, believing you cannot tolerate anxiety and won't be able to cope with anxiety or other unexpected events. More than one of these beliefs may underlie your obsessive fears. These and other interpretations and beliefs that you hold will be the focus of cognitive therapy in the next few sessions.

During exposure, be sure to pay attention to the feared stimulus as much as possible and to use your reactions to the exposure to help figure out your thinking. You may need to continue the exposure after the end of the session to be sure you have processed it fully from an emotional point of view.

Homework

You and your therapist should agree on exposure homework that will be consistent with what you did during session so that any reduction in your discomfort generalizes to other similar settings. You can pass on any special instructions to your family assistant. As always, be sure to prevent any avoidance and any rituals during your homework exposures. Your therapist will ask you to complete a Homework Form. You should also keep a record of any intrusive experiences and your interpretations and assumptions when obsessive fears arise during the week. You can do this during exposure homework and also when unexpected exposures provoke discomfort for you. Use the Thought-Record Form at the end of this chapter to keep this record. Record the situation that provoked the obsessive fear, thought, or image and any thoughts that you noticed in connection with the obsession. To become more aware of your thinking, ask yourself questions like "What am I thinking?" or "What am I worried about?" and write down any ideas that pop into your head. The form also asks you to rate how strongly you believe in your interpretation and then what emotions you experienced, such as anxiety, guilt, anger, sadness, etc., and the strength of these emotional reactions. If you have any questions about how to fill out this form, be sure to discuss it with your therapist.

Cognitive Triangle

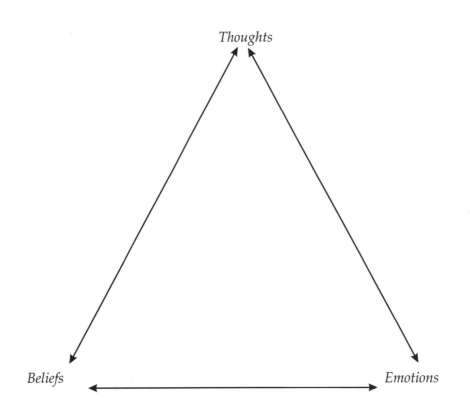

Downward Arrow Form

Interpretation

1.

If that were true, why would it be upsetting? What would it mean to me?

2.

If that were true, why would it be upsetting? What would it mean to me?

3.

If that were true, why would it be upsetting? What would it mean to me?

4.

If that were true, why would it be upsetting? What would it mean to me?

5.

If that were true, why would it be upsetting? What would it mean to me?

6.

Thought-Record Form #1

Name: _____ Date: _____

Situation/Trigger	Intrusion	Interpretation a) write interpretation b) rate belief in interpretation 0–100%	Emotion a) specify anxious, depressed, guilty, etc. b) rate degree of emotion 0–100%

Instructions for Thought-Record Form #1

Situation/Trigger: Describe the actual situation that caused the unpleasant emotion, or describe the series of thoughts, daydreams, or recollections that lead to unpleasant emotion.

Intrusion: Unwanted thought that is uncontrollable and difficult to get rid of

Interpretation: The cognitive reaction that you have to the intrusion

    a) write your interpretation of the intrusive thought

    b) how credible is this thought for you, 0 to 100 percent?

Emotion: Fear, anxiety, sadness, guilt, surprise, etc.

    a) describe which emotion you have

    b) how strong is this emotion, 0 to 100 percent?

Session 8

Exposure and Cognitive Therapy
(Logical Errors and Interpretations)

Agenda

The agenda for this session is identical to the last session with the addition of helping you identify errors in your thinking about obsessions and deliberately examining your interpretations of obsessive intrusions when they occur.

Homework Review

With your therapist, review how the exposure and blocking of rituals and avoidance went since last session. Your therapist may choose to wait to review your Thought-Record Forms assigned last week until after you have begun the exposure from your hierarchy planned for this session.

Exposure and Ritual Prevention

As in the last session, begin exposure to the next item on your hierarchy. Expose yourself as fully as possible and report your discomfort level to your therapist. Pay attention to the situation and to how you feel, but especially notice your thoughts when you are uncomfortable to see how you are interpreting the experience. Your therapist will ask you about these. Once you begin to feel that you can manage the exposure reasonably well, your therapist is likely to begin reviewing your Thought-Record Forms and help you with some cognitive interventions as described below.

Cognitive Therapy

If you were able to apply the downward arrow procedure from last session, it might be useful to apply it now to the exposure you are doing. If that doesn't seem helpful, your therapist may ask you about your interpretations associated with an obsessive situation or event that happened since the last session. Remember that your therapist doesn't know the answers to questions he or she may ask, and there are no right or wrong answers. It is important to examine how you think and what goes through your mind, even if it seems silly or unreasonable. Think of yourself as a scientist trying to study an interesting phenomenon and to report on your observations.

If you had trouble completing the Thought Record Form, please discuss this with your therapist. Otherwise, look it over and try to formulate your interpretations as hypotheses. Hypotheses are "If . . . , then . . ." statements that specify what you think will happen under certain circumstances. For example, after looking at the thoughts you wrote down, you might record your hypothesis as: "If I can't remember this fact, that means I am a stupid person." Now you can examine whether you think that, in fact, your hypothesis is really true. To do this, you will need to decide whether you think it is true of you and also whether you think it is true of all people. You'll also need to think whether it is true only in special situations or whether it is always true. If you think it is true of you, but not of other people, or true sometimes but not others, you will have to consider how these discrepancies could be explained. Think about what evidence you are using to draw your conclusion.

In doing this, you are taking on the role of a scientist to examine your own thinking and the evidence that supports or refutes it. Identifying your interpretations and hypotheses is a skill that takes some practice to master. Once you have learned to do it, there are several ways to examine the evidence to help you decide which interpretations or beliefs are reasonable and which ones you think are mistaken. In this session you will learn to identify cognitive errors you might be making and to challenge your interpretations so you can examine the evidence for your hypotheses carefully.

Cognitive Errors

One way to challenge faulty interpretations is to see whether you are in the habit of thinking in certain sorts of irrational ways. At the end of this chapter, look over the List of Cognitive Errors to see whether any of these are occurring now in the way you are thinking about this exposure situation. For example, are you "labeling" yourself as stupid or engaging in "fortune telling" by blaming yourself already for something bad that hasn't happened without considering the possibility of good outcomes? Sometimes it is helpful to challenge this type of thinking by asking yourself, "What evidence do I have to base this prediction on?" Catastrophizing and emotional reasoning are other common thinking errors. Another is black-and-white thinking, for example, "If I do 'X,' I'll cause serious harm." One way to examine the accuracy of this kind of thinking is to try thinking in shades of gray or percentages: "Exactly how big an opportunity will I miss compared to other opportunities?"

Challenging Interpretations

You and your therapist will be looking for common themes that run through your assumptions and beliefs. Sometimes these can cause mistaken interpretations of obsessive intrusions. Your therapist will try to help you decide which beliefs and interpretations are the most problematic and find cognitive techniques that will be most helpful. To work on this, it may be useful to select a few thoughts from your Thought Record and figure out what themes you can detect. Below is a list of possibilities that are fairly common for people with OCD. Some of these were mentioned in session 3.

- Overimportance of thoughts

- Need to control thoughts and/or actions

- Overestimating the probability or the severity of danger

- Overconcern about certainty or difficulty tolerating ambiguous situations

- Excessive responsibility

- Perfectionism and strict standards for your behavior

- Concern about the consequences of anxiety and/or your ability to cope it

These beliefs often result in faulty interpretations of intrusive thoughts. For example, if you believed that it was important to control your thoughts, you would be more likely to be upset when an unwanted thought occurred because you would interpret this to mean that you were bad and were about to lose control. You and your therapist can begin to look more carefully at your interpretations to see if there are other ways to look at them or other assumptions that might be equally valid. The thought challenging techniques are useful tools to help you develop alternative hypotheses. You can try on or test these alternative explanations in specific exposures or experiments later on.

Challenging your beliefs is not just an exercise; it does lead to real change in attitudes and behavior. If you have doubts about this, chances are that you have already had this experience in another type of context that you and your therapist might discuss. Consider the following questions, which may help you challenge your interpretations and formulate rational alternatives:

- What is the evidence for and against my specific interpretation?

- Are my interpretations logical?

- Have I confused a thought with a fact?

- Are my interpretations of the situation realistic?

- Am I using black-and-white thinking?

- Am I confusing certainties with possibilities?

- Is my judgment based on the way I feel instead of facts?

- Have I emphasized the irrelevant factors?

- What would I tell a friend who told me this?

- What would a friend say to me?

- What could I tell myself?

- What are the advantages and disadvantages of this type of thinking?

- Is this thought helpful right now?

- What would be a more rational way of looking at that?

Homework

You and your therapist should agree on your exposure homework until the next session. You can also plan to listen to taped imagined exposures if these are relevant. You may need to pass any special instructions on to your family assistant if you have one. Remember to anticipate and block avoidance and rituals. Also, your therapist will probably ask you to complete another version of the Thought Record (#2) which includes an additional column for you to write down how you challenged your thoughts and rate how credible were the rational alternatives that you used.

List of Cognitive Errors

1. **All-or-Nothing Thinking:** You see things in black-or-white categories. If a situation falls short of perfect, you see it as a total failure.

2. **Overgeneralization:** You see a single negative event, such as a romantic rejection or a career reversal, as a never-ending pattern of defeat by using words such as "always" or "never" when you think about it.

3. **Mental Filter:** You pick out a single negative detail and dwell on it exclusively, so that your vision of all of reality becomes darkened, like the drop of ink that discolors a beaker of water. Example: You receive many positive comments about your presentation to a group of associates at work, but one of them says something mildly critical. You obsess about his reaction for days and ignore all the positive feedback.

4. **Discounting the Positive:** You reject positive experiences by insisting they "don't count." If you do a good job, you may tell yourself that it wasn't good enough or that anyone could have done as well. Discounting the positive takes the joy out of life and makes you feel inadequate and unrewarded.

5. **Jumping to Conclusions:** You interpret things negatively when there are no facts to support your conclusion. Variations on this theme are:
   - *Mind reading:* Without checking it out, you arbitrarily conclude that someone is reacting negatively to you.
   - *Fortune telling:* You predict that things will turn out badly, even when you don't really know what will happen.

6. **Magnification:** You exaggerate the importance of your problems and shortcomings, or you minimize the importance of your desirable qualities.

7. **Emotional Reasoning:** You assume that your negative emotions necessarily reflect the way things really are: "I feel guilty. I must have done something wrong; I must be a bad person." Or "I feel anxious. Something terrible must be about to happen."

8. **"Should" Statements:** You tell yourself that things should be the way you hoped or expected them to be. "Musts," "oughts," and "have to's" are similar offenders. "Should" statements that are directed against yourself lead to guilt and frustration. "Should" statements directed against other people or the world in general lead to anger and frustration.

Continued on Next Page

9. **Labeling:** Labeling is an extreme form of all-or-nothing thinking. Instead of saying, "I made a mistake," you attach a negative label to yourself: "I'm a loser." You might also label yourself "a fool" or "a failure" or "a jerk." Labeling is quite irrational because you are not the same as what you do. Human beings exist, but "fools," "losers," and "jerks" do not. These labels are just useless abstractions that lead to anger, anxiety, frustration, and low self-esteem.

10. **Personalization and Blame:** Personalization occurs when you hold yourself personally responsible for an event that isn't entirely under your control. Personalization leads to guilt, shame, and feelings of inadequacy. For example, a woman who received a notice that her child was having difficulties at school told herself, "This shows what a bad mother I am," instead of trying to pinpoint the cause of the problem so that she could be helpful to her child.

Adapted from D. Burns. 1989. *Feeling Good Handbook*. Morrow: New York.

Thought-Record Form #2

Name: _____   Date: _____

Situation/Trigger	Intrusion	Interpretation a) write interpretation b) rate belief in interpretation 0-100%	Emotion a) specify anxious, depressed, guilty, etc. b) rate degree of emotion 0–100%	Rational Response a) write rational response to interpretation b) rate belief in rational response 0–100	Outcome a) re-rate belief b) specify and re-rate subsequent emotions

Instructions for Thought-Record Form #2

Situation/Trigger: The actual situation that caused the unpleasant emotion, or describe the series of thoughts, daydreams, or recollections that lead to unpleasant emotion

Intrusion: Unwanted thought that is uncontrollable and difficult to get rid of

Interpretation: The cognitive reaction that you have to the intrusion
  a) write your interpretation of the intrusive thought
  b) how credible is this thought for you, 0 to 100 percent?

Emotion: Fear, anxiety, sadness, guilt, surprise, etc.
  a) specify which emotion you have (fear, guilt, sadness, etc.)
  b) how strong is this emotion, 0 to 100 percent?

Challenges to Intrusions: The answers to these questions might help you formulate a rational response:
  - What is the evidence for and against your specific interpretation?
  - Is your interpretation logical or realistic?
  - Have you confused a thought with a fact?
  - Are you using black-and-white thinking?
  - Are you confusing certainties with possibilities?
  - Is your judgment based on emotion instead of facts?
  - Are you emphasizing the irrelevant factors?
  - What would you tell a friend who said this to you?
  - What would a friend say to you if you told them your thinking?
  - What are the advantages and disadvantages of this type of thinking? Is this thought helpful right now?
  - Is there a more rational way of looking at the situation?

Rational Response:
  a) write rational response to interpretation
  b) how credible is this rational thought, 0 to 100 percent?

Outcome:
  a) how credible is the original automatic thought now, 0 to 100 percent?
  b) what emotions does it cause and how strong are they, 0 to 100 percent?

Session 9

Exposure and Cognitive Therapy
(Overimportance of Thoughts)

Agenda

The agenda for this session will be similar to the last session, with the addition of learning cognitive techniques that may be helpful for challenging interpretations and beliefs about the overimportance of thoughts and the need to control thoughts.

Homework Review

You and your therapist can review the exposure Homework Form and discuss your progress and any difficulties. You will also want to review your Thought Records for this session, either before starting or after you have begun the exposure.

Exposure and Blocking Rituals

Proceed to the next item on your hierarchy list; expose yourself to the situation so that you can process the situation fully. As you work with more difficult items on your list, you may find that you need a little more help managing your anxiety and remaining in the situation. Your therapist will suggest ways to help if this is needed. Pay attention to your emotional reactions and the thoughts, ideas, or images that arise, as well as to your interpretations or beliefs.

Cognitive Therapy

Challenging the Importance of Thoughts

Discuss the ways in which you tried to challenge your interpretations and beliefs on your Thought-Record Form. It is important to try to keep your scientific perspective as much as you can since it helps you examine your reactions more objectively. Be sure that you are focusing on your hypotheses about yourself and not just on the obsessive thoughts. This session contains several suggestions for ways to work on your interpretations, especially if they concern overimportance of thoughts. The main ideas related to overimportance of thoughts are that:

- Just having the thought means it is important.

- Thoughts can cause behaviors or events.

- Thinking is as bad as doing.

Your therapist will help you decide which of the techniques suggested below are likely to be pertinent or useful in your situation.

Examining the Logic

If you think that "If I have a thought, it must be important," you and your therapist can discuss whether you think that all of your thoughts are important just because you think them. That is, are some of your thoughts unimportant?

If you think that "Thoughts can cause actions," you and your therapist can try generating other examples of this besides your usual obsessive thought to see whether you believe this is true in situations besides your obsessive ones. Sometimes you may need to test your ideas by using a behavioral experiment during the coming week.

If you think that "Thinking is the same as doing," consider again the fact that 85 to 90 percent of ordinary people have intrusive thoughts which may be similar to your own. These were listed in table 1 in the introduction. You and your therapist might want to examine the likelihood that you would act on your ideas, as well as the kind of evidence you would consider appropriate to determine whether someone who has these kind of thoughts would act on them. You may wish to discuss any learning experiences you have had that might contribute to your beliefs.

Survey Method

Sometimes it may be useful to take a different perspective for a while. For example, you might ask yourself whether you would hold the same attitude toward someone else you know well. You might also want to conduct a small survey among people you know to determine how different your thoughts are from a group of people without OCD.

Continuum Technique

If you think of yourself as "bad" or "immoral" because of obsessive thoughts, such as harming others or engaging in sexual acts, it may be useful to rate your own behavior in relation to other "bad" or "immoral" acts. Your therapist can help you examine your attitudes about yourself in the context of your beliefs about all immoral acts. For example, you could draw a line and write "extremely immoral" at one end and "very moral" at the other end. Decide what behavior belongs at each extreme, as well as in the middle. Rate "thinking about (your thought)" in comparison to other actions you listed.

Advantages and Disadvantages

Your therapist can also help you examine and list the pros and cons of your interpretations and beliefs so you can examine the value of the advantages compared to the disadvantages.

Challenging the Need to Control Thoughts

Many people with OCD try to manage their anxiety by trying to control their obsessive thoughts. If this is true for you, it may be useful to learn the effects of trying to stop your obsessive thoughts. Use the Thought Suppression Graph given at the end of this session to graph how often the obsessive thought occurs on days when you try to stop it compared to days when you allow it to appear freely without interference. It is usually best to alternate suppression days with no interference days to see the effect.

Homework

Agree on your exposure homework until the next session and plan to listen to taped imagined exposures, if these are relevant. Remember to anticipate and block avoidance and rituals. Continue completing the Thought-Record Form and note whenever you tried one of the methods you learned in this session or previous ones. After trying out the methods you are taught, select the ones you find most useful or comfortable and use these as often as it seems appropriate.

Thought Suppression Graph

Number of intrusions

Day 1   Day 2   Day 3   Day 4   Day 5   Day 6   Day 7

Intrusive thought to suppress:

_____

_____

_____

Session 10

Exposure and Cognitive Therapy
(Danger and Anxiety)

Agenda

The agenda for this session is similar to previous ones, with the addition of challenging interpretations and beliefs about overestimation of the probability or severity of danger and the consequences of experiencing anxiety.

Homework Review

You and your therapist should review the exposure homework, as well as your Thought Records to see how you are applying the cognitive-therapy skills you have learned so far. You and your therapist can also review the Thought Suppression Graph if you used this during the week.

Exposure and Ritual Prevention

For many OCD sufferers, exposure sessions will occur outside the office or may be assigned mainly as homework if the therapist cannot be present. Remember to be in full contact with your next hierarchy item or situations. Observe your emotions, thoughts, and behaviors and take care not to allow any rituals or avoidance of this situation. Discuss with your therapist your catastrophic fears and any other emotional reactions and interpretations or beliefs that you experience.

Cognitive Therapy

Your therapist will want to know which cognitive skills you have found helpful since the last session and whether you noticed any cognitive errors and how you dealt with these. Several additional cognitive techniques are described below as possible options for you and your therapist to consider, depending on the nature of your obsessive symptoms and beliefs.

Challenging Estimates of Harmful Outcomes

If you are prone to overestimating danger, you may want to actually *calculate the probability of the dangerous outcome*. To do this, you will need to first determine what specific events would have to occur to lead to the outcome you fear, estimate actual likelihood of each event separately, and compute the overall chances of the feared harm by multiplying together all of the chances of each separate event. You can then compare your original estimate of the probability to the one you calculate after thinking it through carefully. Your therapist can work this through with you.

The *survey method* that was described in session 9 may also be useful to determine the frequency or likelihood of your feared consequences. First make a prediction about the likelihood of the outcome you fear and then find out how many people actually experienced this event and what their attitude would be toward people who make this mistake. You may notice that you tend to estimate a greater likelihood of harm or danger when you're anxious than when you are calm. Consider how you might use this information when you are confronted with your obsessive fears between sessions.

Another method for examining the accuracy of your predictions about the probability of catastrophes is *behavioral experiments*. These are like scientific experiments to test the evidence for and against alternate interpretations. Your therapist will help you devise experiments that test your hypotheses, and you can record your experiences on the Cognitive-Behavioral Experiment Form at the end of this chapter. As a general rule, for all of your experiments you should first specify in writing the hypothesis you are testing (that is, the likelihood of occurrence of feared consequences) and also review that hypothesis after you've completed the experiment.

Challenging Estimations of the Severity of the Consequences

If your therapist agrees that it would be useful, you may wish to *consult with an expert* to determine whether the consequences of a feared outcome will be as severe as you expect. Be sure, however, that this is not just another way to obtain reassurance that is like doing a ritual. Also, consulting with an expert should not be a substitute for examining whether you are making important cognitive errors, like jumping to conclusions or black-and-white thinking. If you notice this, ask yourself whether this type of thinking is also appropriate for other contexts in which other types of disasters (not your obsessive ones) might occur. Your therapist can help you do this. You may also need to ask yourself whether the fact that a disaster could occur and would be terrible makes it any more likely.

Role playing or the *courtroom technique* may help you generate alternate hypotheses besides your catastrophic ones. You can test these by playing the role of a judge or jury member or acting as a lawyer in your own case. You will need to evaluate the rationality of the arguments you have been making from a new perspective in which only reasonable evidence is admissible in "court." See session 11 for more detail about this method.

Challenging Beliefs About the Consequences of Anxiety

Some OCD sufferers believe that anxiety is dangerous or that it will render them unable to function. These types of beliefs can interfere with exposure because people who are afraid of experiencing discomfort often use rituals and avoidance to stop or control anxiety. This, in turn, prevents them from disconfirming these and other faulty beliefs and interpretations. Sufferers with these fears may worry about the immediate effects of anxiety, for example, going crazy or losing control of your senses. If you have these types of beliefs, your therapist can help you use the *downward arrow technique* to identify your fears and associated beliefs. You and your therapist can then review whether you ever felt anxious in the way you've feared in the past and what happened when you did. Consider whether you have ever lost control or behaved strangely if you fear these outcomes.

Some people with OCD believe that anxiety will prevent them from functioning. If this is a problem for you, consider whether you have been anxious in the past but still functioned, even if you weren't at your best. If this is true for you, you will need to reevaluate the accuracy of your belief that functioning with anxiety is impossible. If you are afraid of anxiety in the future, your therapist can help you explore whether trying to avoid anxiety by using rituals and avoidance is actually likely to reduce your obsessive fear. As you think about what has happened on previous occasions when you tried to avoid anxiety, you and your therapist can examine the *advantages and disadvantages* of continuing your OCD behavior.

Behavioral experiments can also be used to challenge overestimates of the negative consequences of anxiety. You and your therapist can write down your predictions about your behavior while you are anxious in certain situations and then agree on an assignment to test this prediction by observing your actual performance while you are anxious. Then you can compare your prediction to your actual performance and develop a hypothesis to explain what happened.

Homework

Your exposure homework will be similar to last session's, but with new items that are next on your hierarchy. You can also follow cognitive therapy homework assignments that you and your therapist agree on by using the techniques you have learned so far. These include using the downward arrow to identify your worst fears and basic beliefs, examining the evidence from a scientific or courtroom perspective, generating alternative hypotheses, conducting surveys, evaluating your own behavior on the entire continuum of problem behaviors that you obsess about, calculating the probability of danger and challenging your estimations of consequences of anxiety, and examining the advantages and disadvantages. Finally, you and your therapist can agree on which behavioral experiments should be carried out.

Cognitive-Behavioral Experiment Form

Session # _____ Name _____ Date _____

1. Behavioral experiment to be completed:

_____

_____

_____

2. Feared consequences (what do you predict will happen?):

_____

_____

3. Strength of belief in the feared consequences (from 0–100%) _____

4. Degree of anxiety or discomfort (0–100): Beginning _____ End _____

5. Consequences that actually happened:

_____

_____

6. Did your predictions come true?

_____

_____

7. How did you challenge your feared consequence/predictions?

_____

_____

_____

8. Was the thought challenging helpful? (If not, why not?)

_____

_____

Exposure and Cognitive Therapy
(Responsibility)

Agenda

The agenda for this session is similar to previous ones, with the addition of cognitive techniques for challenging interpretations and beliefs about responsibility for thoughts and actions and the consequences of responsibility. Exposure and cognitive homework will be assigned.

Homework Review

You and your therapist should review the exposure homework, as well as your Thought Records to see how you are applying the cognitive therapy skills you have learned so far. You and your therapist can also review the Cognitive-Behavioral Experiment Form if you used it during the week.

Exposure and Ritual Prevention

Exposure should continue as before, scheduling sessions in or outside the office as needed or as homework if the therapist cannot be present. By now you should be working on the highest items on the hierarchy and it is very important to be in full contact with these hierarchy situations. Observe your emotions, thoughts, and behaviors and do not allow any rituals or avoidance of the situations you are working on. Discuss with your therapist your catastrophic fears and any other emotional reactions and interpretations or beliefs that you experience. Continue the exposures until your discomfort reduces noticeably.

Cognitive Therapy

This session includes some additional methods for working on problems you might have with overestimating your responsibility for your thoughts and actions. As for the previous sessions, some of these problems and ways of resolving them will not fit for you. You and your therapist can pick and choose what seems to be most relevant and likely to have the most benefit for you.

Challenging Responsibility

Some OCD sufferers believe that they are responsible for having an obsessive thought that makes them uncomfortable (for example, thoughts about stabbing someone or blasphemous thoughts) or that they are responsible for doing or not doing something (for example, not picking up objects in the road to prevent someone from having an accident or failing to check something). People who have these kinds of obsessive fears often feel guilty and fear that others will reject them if they find out that they have been "irresponsible" in these ways. If you experience obsessive fears like these and tend to believe that it is your responsibility to control your thoughts and actions, the treatment methods suggested below may be of help. Consult with your therapist about how best to use these methods.

Pie Technique

One way to work on changing your beliefs about responsibility is to use the pie technique. First, estimate what percentage of responsibility you believe you have for what you are afraid will happen. Then, with your therapist's help make a written list of all of the other factors that could possibly play a role. Often there are some that you have not thought of because you are so focused on your own role in the potential problem. Your therapist can help you think about this and a supportive family member might also be helpful. Then, draw all of these portions of responsibility as pieces of a pie. Label all of the pieces and make them larger or smaller depending on the amount of responsibility they should have for the outcome you are concerned about. Draw your own contribution last. After you are finished, see how your original estimate of your responsibility compares to the one after you have finished the pie.

Courtroom Approach

You can also use the courtroom technique described in session 10 to challenge your interpretations of responsibility. You and your therapist can decide which roles to play first, but eventually, you must attempt to defend your guilt using only empirical evidence that would be allowed in a court of law. This means that emotional reasoning in which you are accused of being guilty simply because you feel that way would not be considered acceptable evidence unless you can generate factual proof. Your therapist will help remind you when evidence would be inadmissible. You may need to use this method several times for various obsessive fears before you are able to use it to challenge your irrational interpretations when you are alone.

Double-Standard Technique

Many OCD sufferers hold one standard of responsibility for themselves but another for other people. Often their expectation of blame from others is much greater than their own blame of someone else who might contribute to or cause the same problem. If this double standard applies to you, your therapist can help you evaluate what you actually believe and why. You might also want to consider the advantages and disadvantages (or costs and benefits) of maintaining a double standard.

Behavioral Experiments

Experiments can also help you correct beliefs about being overly responsible. As usual, you can write out your hypotheses and predictions first and after doing the experiment, you can examine whether your predictions came true and whether there are any alternative hypotheses. Your therapist will help you design experiments if this method seems useful for you.

Homework

Your exposure homework should follow what you worked on in this session or since the last assignment. Consider whether you will need any family assistance or discussion, and how you will prevent rituals and avoidance. Complete the Thought Record during planned or unexpected exposure situations, and apply relevant cognitive techniques taught so far, after discussing your preferences with your therapist. These techniques include the ones learned in previous sessions, as well as those described for this session to resolve problems with excessive responsibility. These include the pie technique, courtroom approach, double-standard examination, and possibly behavioral experiments. At the next session let your therapist know which methods you used and which ones worked best.

Exposure and Cognitive Therapy
(Certainty and Perfectionism)

Agenda

The agenda for this session is similar to previous ones, with the addition of cognitive techniques for challenging interpretations and beliefs about the need for certainty and perfectionism. Exposure and cognitive homework will be assigned.

Homework Review

You and your therapist should review the exposure homework, as well as your Thought Records and the Cognitive-Behavioral Experiment Form, if applicable, to see how you are applying the cognitive therapy skills you have learned so far.

Exposure and Ritual Prevention

At this point, you should have been exposed to the highest items on your hierarchy. From this point on, you will need to continue exposures to items that are still difficult and provoke the most discomfort. You and your therapist should review the original hierarchy so you can give new discomfort ratings to each item to determine what exposures are still needed. Some or all of these may need to occur outside the office and as homework assignments, as in previous sessions. Try to work in a variety of different exposure contexts to encourage generalization of your gains to multiple settings. Your therapist will want you to take the primary lead in planning the exposures if you have not already begun to do this, so that you are prepared to handle future situations when obsessions or compulsive urges occur when you are not in treatment. You and your therapist can also review the Thought Records and discuss the techniques that were most helpful.

Cognitive Therapy

Challenging the Need for Certainty and Perfectionism

Some OCD sufferers have problems with a need for certainty and difficulty tolerating ambiguous situations. If you think this is a problem for you, sometimes the *downward arrow* method can help clarify exactly what you fear most, if this is not already apparent to you and your therapist. In using this method of specifying each part of the fear, notice whether you are making any cognitive errors. Common ones are *black-and-white thinking* and *jumping to conclusions*, but you may also have others. Consider whether these thoughts are reasonable in the context you have outlined.

Another useful method already described is examining the *advantages and disadvantages* of being certain or being perfect and meeting high standards. As you do this, consider the value of the advantages and also examine the disadvantages of being certain or perfect. Usually, these are substantial and may be what brought you into treatment.

The *survey method* also may be helpful in challenging the need for certainty or meeting perfectionistic standards. Consider conducting a survey of a small group of people about their own standards and certainty in various situations that you and your therapist think would be good tests. It is best to first predict how you think the survey will turn out and then compare your predictions to the actual results.

The *continuum technique* was used previously for overimportance of thoughts and may be helpful here. On paper you can create a scale from least to most important with regard to certainty and perfectionistic standards and decide what to put at each end as a good description of the ends of your scale. Your therapist can help you decide what goes there. Then, think where on this scale you would put different examples of situations on the continuum you are working on. After this, rate the most recent situation when you were concerned about certainty or standards and see how it compares with your attitude at the time of that obsessive concern.

For example, you might create the following scale:

not important to
remember/be
certain

very important to
remember/be
certain

Consider where an item like remembering who pitched for the Yankees in 1950 would fit on this scale. What about remembering your children's birthdates? Now, rate your most recent intrusive thought about forgetting or uncertainty. Where does it fall on the scale? Often, it is also helpful to enumerate all of the things (not just obsessive ones) that you aren't certain about and examine the need to know these things as well.

You could also design a *behavioral experiment* to challenge the importance of certainty and whether failing to know something or meet a certain standard means that something bad will happen. For example, you might decide to test how you experience doing something mostly right, but not perfectly, like leaving some dishes undone or completing most but not all parts of a task. Work out the details of this experiment with your therapist.

Homework

For homework, plan to do exposure and response prevention to cover the remaining items or situations that still provoke discomfort. You should decide how to conduct these exposures and prevent avoidance by yourself, only asking for help if you feel confused about how to proceed. Plan to complete the Thought-Record Forms and to apply the cognitive techniques you have found useful. If it is a problem for you, challenge your need for certainty and perfectionistic attitudes wherever you see an opportunity. You can report next time which techniques you tried and which ones worked best.

Continuing Exposure and Cognitive Therapy

Agenda

The agenda for these final exposure sessions is the same as previous ones, with the addition of beginning to return to normal behavior if your OCD symptoms disrupted everyday tasks and of doing these tasks on your own without therapist or family assistance. Focus on applying cognitive techniques using methods you have found useful.

Homework Review

You and your therapist should review the exposure Homework Form as well as Thought Records from this week and discuss progress and any problems you encountered.

Exposure and Ritual Prevention

During these two sessions, you and your therapist can plan exposures to any items from the hierarchy that continue to bother you. Sometimes treatment participants notice that some obsessive concerns that have not bothered them recently are now more disturbing. This is not a cause for concern, but you and your therapist will need to plan exposures to these new situations. Review your original hierarchy to decide what exposures you think are still needed. Try to do these as homework self-exposure as much as possible so you get plenty of experience planning and doing your own exposures. Think about any new situations that might present a challenge for you and try to include these in your last sessions or homework assignments.

You will also want to gradually replace the total blocking of rituals required for exposure and ritual-prevention treatment with normal behavior whenever this is appropriate. If you have had washing or cleaning rituals, this means learning to do washing and cleaning tasks in a normal, nonritualistic way. Most OCD sufferers with other types of rituals like checking, ordering, and repeating rituals will not need to do anything different now to achieve normal behavior. However, if you have checking rituals, there may be some instances in which ordinary people would check once but not more often, so you may have to practice normal checking instead of ritualistic checking. Discuss this with your therapist to decide what to do.

Cognitive Therapy

You and your therapist can use your Thought Records to continue to work on cognitive problems using any of the several techniques you have already learned and found helpful. Sometimes you may need to brainstorm to find ways to resolve problematic interpretations and assumptions. Below are listed the types of erroneous interpretations and beliefs we have described earlier:

- Overimportance of thoughts

- Need to control thoughts and/or actions

- Overestimating the probability or the severity of danger

- Concern about the consequences of anxiety and/or your ability to cope with it

- Excessive responsibility

- Overconcern about certainty or difficulty tolerating ambiguous situations

- Perfectionism and strict standards for your behavior

If you are still having problems with some of these, go back to the session in which the cognitive therapy methods that may be useful are discussed.

You have learned several different kinds of methods to help correct errors in your thinking about your OCD symptoms. These are listed below to remind you of methods that might be useful:

- Downward arrow to identify assumptions

- Identifying cognitive errors

- Challenging questions

- Survey method

- Continuum technique

- Listing the advantages and disadvantages

- Thought-suppression test

- Calculating the probability of danger

- Behavioral experiments
- Role playing
- Pie technique
- Courtroom approach
- Double-standard technique

To review any of these refer to earlier sessions where they were described.

Homework

Your exposure and ritual-prevention homework should address remaining items that provoke discomfort for you. Work on these on your own as much as you are able. Continue to complete the Thought Record and apply useful cognitive techniques taught so far.

Session 15

Relapse Prevention

Agenda

The agenda for this session includes homework review, planning exposure and response-prevention homework, discussion of the ending of treatment, and training to prevent a relapse of OCD symptoms.

Homework Review

This is the same as for previous sessions.

Ending Treatment

You will be finishing treatment soon and your therapist may have already scheduled a follow-up appointment. If you have concerns about stopping treatment, or if you anticipate problems, discuss these with your therapist.

Preventing Relapse

After treatment ends, many OCD sufferers do experience some instances of intrusive thoughts (remember this is normal for most people) or even uncontrollable urges to ritualize that disturb them. This is not unusual and is not a cause for alarm. However, to help you prevent your OCD symptoms from returning in the future and causing distress and interference in your life, you will need to anticipate and prepare to handle potentially problematic situations. We call this relapse-prevention training, and it consists of several components:

- Learning to anticipate stressors and risky situations

- Correcting faulty beliefs and assumptions

- Self-exposure training

- Seeking family support and assistance

- Planning lifestyle changes

These skills are described in this session and the next.

Anticipating Stressors and High Risk Situations

It is very possible to live a life with minimal or no interference from OCD symptoms, but this kind of long-term gain requires perseverance and commitment to your personal goals. It is important to expect that your progress on OCD symptoms will not always be smooth and steady. Ups and downs are likely to happen in the coming months and may mean that you are having a lapse, but this is different from a relapse. A *lapse* is a temporary period in which some obsessions, compulsion, or avoidance behaviors return. This usually means that something stressful is going on in your life, and you need to pay attention to it to keep the stressor from affecting other areas of your life. Now is a good time to develop a list with your therapist of potentially stressful situations and hassles that might provoke obsessions or compulsions. Typical examples are interpersonal conflicts, extra responsibilities, fatigue or illness, a job change, media information about a new source of harm, or a serious loss. As you list potential candidates for exacerbating your OCD, consider what cognitive errors or mistaken assumptions you are most likely to make if these events occur.

Practicing Stress Management

When stressful events occur and cause you to be more anxious or worried than usual, like all people, you will need to have some coping skills to get through difficult periods. Without such skills, you are likely to turn to rituals because they used to help you feel better, even if this new stressor has little to do with your old obsessions. To prevent a recurrence of compulsive behavior, now is a good time to learn about stress management techniques that appeal to you and fit your lifestyle. Consider finding one of the many good books available or attending a class on this topic and beginning to incorporate some of the suggestions into your schedule. Examples include relaxation skills, meditation techniques, exercise, planned relaxing activities, and many others. Learning these strategies in advance can help prevent recurrence of serious OCD symptoms.

Correcting Faulty Beliefs and Assumptions

It may be helpful for you to review the cognitive-behavioral model described in session 3 to remind yourself of the principles you've been using during therapy.

You have learned a variety of skills during this treatment program, rather like having a toolbox full of tools that you can use when you need them. The basic steps you've used in the cognitive part of your treatment include:

- Assess your distress levels in feared obsessive situations.

- Identify your faulty interpretations of obsessions or intrusions.

- Write down your interpretations and challenge them.

- Generate alternative interpretations using various methods.

- Test your alternative interpretations using behavioral experiments.

- Compare the results to the predicted results.

Make a list of the cognitive errors you are prone to that you have worked on during treatment. Also make a list of cognitive techniques that have worked well so far to help you challenge your mistaken attitudes. If you notice in the future that your intrusive thoughts and interpretations become troublesome, try self-monitoring them as you did during treatment. Refer to the List of Cognitive Errors and challenging questions from the Thought Record instructions to help you correct faulty thinking. If you've had difficulty identifying exactly what you're afraid of, the downward arrow technique may be helpful in figuring this out. Think about how you could conduct behavioral experiments to test predictions. You and your therapist can write down a list of techniques that you can use in case of recurrence of obsessions in future. If you tend to overestimate the importance of your intrusive thoughts or your responsibility for thoughts or events, refer to the sessions that describe treatments for these problems and include the ones you prefer in your list. You will also need to work on any perfectionistic attitudes you may hold to keep them from contributing to future difficulties.

Fear of Positive Experiences

We have noticed that some people with OCD avoid enjoyable experiences because they associate enjoyment with intrusive obsessions. However, to learn a new lifestyle, it is important to be able to relax and have fun to offset the stresses in your life. It is also important to build some flexibility into your life if you tend to live by strict rules. If these are problems for you, discuss how you might work on this with your therapist. For example, you may be able to design some behavioral experiments to help.

Self-Exposure Training

From now on, you will need to plan any exposure experiences on your own, without your therapist present. It is important to do this before treatment ends, so that you're assured that you can do exposures alone if a particular obsession begins to bother you again. If you need help working on the distinction between normal behavior and rituals, discuss this further with your therapist and develop a plan. If you have noticed any new obsessions, remember that this is common and you should plan exposures for these situations, keeping a record of your anxiety during the exposure.

Seeking Family Support and Assistance

You and your therapist should decide whether to invite your relative(s) to attend these final sessions of treatment to agree upon a plan for support if you experience a lapse in OCD symptoms. It may be helpful for your family to have realistic expectations about future OCD symptoms and to know how to assist if lapses occur. They may also be helpful in identifying non-obsessive activities that would help you return to a normal lifestyle. If you have been living with family members but this does not seem like a good long-term plan, you and your therapist can consider what to do about this and discuss it with your family.

Planning Lifestyle Changes

You and your therapist will want to devote some of this session and the next to discussing important changes in lifestyle, such as working, doing more social activities, and taking on more home responsibilities. Decide what tasks should be accomplished now or after therapy ends to make progress on your goals in living.

Homework

If you need to do any final exposures, cognitive homework, or other homework assignment before your next and final session, decide what tasks need to be done and write these down. Your therapist may ask you to complete some forms like those you answered at the beginning of treatment, along with a questionnaire about your satisfaction with this treatment program.

Session 16

Relapse Prevention and Ending Treatment

Agenda

The agenda for this session includes homework review, discussion of the ending of treatment, and planning for the future.

Homework Review

You and your therapist can review your homework and decide what else you may wish to do after the therapy ends.

Ending Treatment

Your therapist will ask you how you feel about your experience during treatment and how you feel about stopping. You might want to review this treatment manual to remind yourself of the methods your worked on during the therapy. If you haven't already done so, you may want to make up a list to keep in this manual of the specific interventions you found most useful. These are what you will need to refer as a reminder of what to do in stressful times if OCD symptoms reappear.

Plan for the Future

Make sure that you know the likely early warning signs of potential OCD problems and how you will respond to these. Decide what role your family members should play in helping you identify or work on resolving problems, and discuss this with them to get their agreement. You will also want to develop a clear plan to address any problems you have had in functioning at work, and in family, social, and leisure activities. You and your therapist can decide if you need a referral to other agencies for help with other problems like vocational testing, job training, marital therapy, social-skills training, joining ongoing groups, or finding leisure activities of interest.

Support Groups

Many OCD sufferers benefit from continued support from others who have suffered from OCD or from involvement in a support group organization such as a local Obsessive Compulsive Foundation affiliate. These connections can meet several needs. They provide social support in stressful times and social contact for enjoyment; they may occupy free time when you might be tempted to do rituals and also serve as a worthy cause for you to invest your energy in. You and your therapist can decide whether joining a support group or starting one is a good idea. Your therapist can help you find such a group and you may also want to contact the national OC Foundation (listed in the appendix) for information on OCD and on support groups in your area.

Medication Issues

You and your therapist can discuss your plans regarding medication changes if any. If you are considering changing your medications, it may be best to wait for about six months after therapy has ended before deciding to do this to be sure you have stabilized your gains. Sometimes reducing medication too quickly can precipitate a lapse or an episode of depression and so if you do decide to discontinue, a gradual tapering off under your psychiatrist's supervision is wise. Your therapist and your psychiatrist should discuss your options to be sure they are in agreement.

Other Treatment

Many people with OCD also suffer from other kinds of symptoms. Some of these were mentioned in the Introduction, like other anxiety disorders, depression, or Tourette's syndrome. If you suffer from these or other psychological problems, or if you are experiencing other difficulties like marital or parent-child problems, you may want to obtain a referral for other treatment. Ask your therapist about this to decide what to do or whom to see.

Follow-up Assessment and Boosters

You and your therapist may want to schedule meetings at some time in the future and you should probably agree on a plan in case you want to consult your therapist before then. Some people find that booster sessions are useful in the case of a lapse, and these can be arranged as needed if the occasion arises. If you have followed the procedures in this manual and your therapist's recommendations, you should be well on your way to recovery and have the tools to resolve obsessive and compulsive problems as they arise. Enjoy the success your hard work has earned you!

Appendix

Suggested Readings on OCD

Informational Books About OCD

Hollander, E., and D. J. Stein, eds. 1997. *Obsessive Compulsive Disorders*. New York: Marcel Dekker, Inc.

Jenike, M. A., L. Baer, and W. E. Minichiello, eds. 1998. *Obsessive Compulsive Disorder: Practical Management*. Chicago: Mosby.

Swinson, R. P., M. M. Antony, S. Rachman, and M. A. Richter, eds. 1998. *Obsessive-Compulsive Disorder: Theory, Research and Treatment*. New York: Guilford.

Books for OCD Sufferers and Their Families

Baer, L. 1991. *Getting Control*. Lexington, Mass.: Little, Brown & Co.

Foa, E. B., and R. Wilson. 1991. *Stop Obsessing!* New York: Bantam.

Steketee, G., and K. White. 1990. *When Once Is Not Enough*. Oakland, Calif.: New Harbinger.

Sources for Information on OCD

OC Foundation, Inc., P.O. Box 70, Milford, CT 06460-0070; phone: 203-878-5669; fax: 203-874-2826. (For information about OCD and related conditions, about treatment, for referrals and for support group information.)

Obsessive Compulsive Information Center, Madison Institute of Medicine, 7617 Mineral Point Rd., Madison, WI 53717; phone: 608-827-2470; fax: 608-827-2479. (For articles and published information about OCD and treatments.)

Some Other New Harbinger Self-Help Titles

Multiple Chemical Sensitivity: A Survival Guide, $16.95
Dancing Naked, $14.95
Why Are We Still Fighting, $15.95
From Sabotage to Success, $14.95
Parkinson's Disease and the Art of Moving, $15.95
A Survivor's Guide to Breast Cancer, $13.95
Men, Women, and Prostate Cancer, $15.95
Make Every Session Count: Getting the Most Out of Your Brief Therapy, $10.95
Virtual Addiction, $12.95
After the Breakup, $13.95
Why Can't I Be the Parent I Want to Be?, $12.95
The Secret Message of Shame, $13.95
The OCD Workbook, $18.95
Tapping Your Inner Strength, $13.95
Binge No More, $14.95
When to Forgive, $12.95
Practical Dreaming, $12.95
Healthy Baby, Toxic World, $15.95
Making Hope Happen, $14.95
I'll Take Care of You, $12.95
Survivor Guilt, $14.95
Children Changed by Trauma, $13.95
Understanding Your Child's Sexual Behavior, $12.95
The Self-Esteem Companion, $10.95
The Gay and Lesbian Self-Esteem Book, $13.95
Making the Big Move, $13.95
How to Survive and Thrive in an Empty Nest, $13.95
Living Well with a Hidden Disability, $15.95
Overcoming Repetitive Motion Injuries the Rossiter Way, $15.95
What to Tell the Kids About Your Divorce, $13.95
The Divorce Book, Second Edition, $15.95
Claiming Your Creative Self: True Stories from the Everyday Lives of Women, $15.95
Six Keys to Creating the Life You Desire, $19.95
Taking Control of TMJ, $13.95
What You Need to Know About Alzheimer's, $15.95
Winning Against Relapse: A Workbook of Action Plans for Recurring Health and Emotional Problems, $14.95
Facing 30: Women Talk About Constructing a Real Life and Other Scary Rites of Passage, $12.95
The Worry Control Workbook, $15.95
Wanting What You Have: A Self-Discovery Workbook, $18.95
When Perfect Isn't Good Enough: Strategies for Coping with Perfectionism, $13.95
Earning Your Own Respect: A Handbook of Personal Responsibility, $12.95
High on Stress: A Woman's Guide to Optimizing the Stress in Her Life, $13.95
Infidelity: A Survival Guide, $13.95
Stop Walking on Eggshells, $14.95
Consumer's Guide to Psychiatric Drugs, $16.95
The Fibromyalgia Advocate: Getting the Support You Need to Cope with Fibromyalgia and Myofascial Pain, $18.95
Healing Fear: New Approaches to Overcoming Anxiety, $16.95
Working Anger: Preventing and Resolving Conflict on the Job, $12.95
Sex Smart: How Your Childhood Shaped Your Sexual Life and What to Do About It, $14.95
You Can Free Yourself From Alcohol & Drugs, $13.95
Amongst Ourselves: A Self-Help Guide to Living with Dissociative Identity Disorder, $14.95
Healthy Living with Diabetes, $13.95
Dr. Carl Robinson's Basic Baby Care, $10.95
Better Boundries: Owning and Treasuring Your Life, $13.95
Goodbye Good Girl, $12.95
Fibromyalgia & Chronic Myofascial Pain Syndrome, $19.95
The Depression Workbook: Living With Depression and Manic Depression, $17.95
Self-Esteem, Second Edition, $13.95
Angry All the Time: An Emergency Guide to Anger Control, $12.95
When Anger Hurts, $13.95
Perimenopause, $16.95
The Relaxation & Stress Reduction Workbook, Fourth Edition, $17.95
The Anxiety & Phobia Workbook, Second Edition, $18.95
I Can't Get Over It, A Handbook for Trauma Survivors, Second Edition, $16.95
Messages: The Communication Skills Workbook, Second Edition, $15.95
Thoughts & Feelings, Second Edition, $18.95
Depression: How It Happens, How It's Healed, $14.95
The Deadly Diet, Second Edition, $14.95
The Power of Two, $15.95
Living Without Depression & Manic Depression: A Workbook for Maintaining Mood Stability, $18.95
Couple Skills: Making Your Relationship Work, $14.95
Hypnosis for Change: A Manual of Proven Techniques, Third Edition, $15.95

Call **toll free, 1-800-748-6273,** or log on to our online bookstore at **www.newharbinger.com** to order. Have your Visa or Mastercard number ready. Or send a check for the titles you want to New Harbinger Publications, Inc., 5674 Shattuck Ave., Oakland, CA 94609. Include $3.80 for the first book and 75¢ for each additional book, to cover shipping and handling. (California residents please include appropriate sales tax.) Allow two to five weeks for delivery.

Prices subject to change without notice.